defending our lives

defending our lives

GETTING AWAY FROM DOMESTIC VIOLENCE AND STAYING SAFE

susan murphy-milano

ANCHOR BOOKS
DOUBLEDAY

NEW YORK LONDON TORONTO SYDNEY AUCKLAND

AN ANCHOR BOOK

PUBLISHED BY DOUBLEDAY

a division of Bantam Doubleday Dell Publishing Group, Inc.
1540 Broadway, New York, New York 10036

ANCHOR BOOKS, DOUBLEDAY, and the portrayal of an anchor
are trademarks of Doubleday, a division of
Bantam Doubleday Dell Publishing Group, Inc.

Book design by Susan Yuran

Library of Congress Cataloging-in-Publication Data
Murphy-Milano, Susan.
Defending our lives : getting away from domestic violence and
staying safe / Susan Murphy-Milano.
p.   cm.
1. Abused women—Services for—United States.   2. Abused women—
Legal status, laws, etc.—United States.   3. Wife abuse—
Investigation—United States.   4. Family violence—United States.
5. Women's shelters—United States.   I. Title.
HV6626.2.M87   1996
362.82'92—dc20   96-16417
CIP

ISBN 0-385-48441-0

Printed in the United States of America

First Anchor Books Edition: October 1996

1   3   5   7   9   10   8   6   4   2

contents

contents

contents

This woman given long of nothing,
but a chance to give of herself,
but still they beat and asked for more.
As always she accepted with a
face that never broke.

In the struggle to find the hidden way to love,
herself she lost!
But she found a way through kind and good
to give to every other
and only asked to see the start of a smile.

And I who blossomed strong and late have worked
and spoke and prayed so long to make her proud,
now in the memories of her far
but still not absent ways,
I chose to simply ease her thoughts in anytime
of anxious pain
in the moving moments of a gift of rhyme.

And I shall offer her my always love,
although I know and hate and fear,

that my forever words are not enough.
And with new words I offer love so late
but still so dear.

Mama, you on this day shall always keep,
this giving praising moment of each thought
and gift,
though to all other moments when they forgot
when you were only always there.

On this day although a great tragedy,
you are being bestowed the greatest honor
one can obtain,
that is of love, family, and friends.

You fought long and hard of all of your adult life,
we understand that this is God's way of making
the rest of your days that of peace, joy, and
harmony that you never demanded
but rightfully deserved.

She paid the price of victory with her life.
Maybe it was for all those who remain silent and
suffered unheard.
I pray we will better understand our tragic loss
and forgive those who turned away,
rest assured, Mama,
we will continue to fight
and you will not be among
the silent but victorious!

—susan murphy-milano

acknowledgments

I am grateful to the Reverend Yvonne M. Christman, who took this wounded bird and made it possible for me to soar through the universe. To Presiding Juvenile Court Judge Nancy Sidote Salyers, for believing I could make a difference and for always lending an ear. To M. Susan Raef for your encouragement and inspiration no matter what the time of day or night.

Thanks as well to the entire Chicago media, each and every one of you, for allowing my voice to be heard in order to help others.

Special thanks to Denise Hahn, Veronica Robinson, Char Crotty, Ann Breen-Greco, Diane Murphy, Sonny Fisher, Sam Ballin, Ora Schub, Yolonda Rivorsa, and Estelle Beck, for guiding, directing, and supporting me and all of my efforts through the years, unconditionally.

I would also like to express my appreciation to my editor, Arabella Meyer, for taking on this project. You've helped make a long-awaited dream a reality. You are a terrific teacher and this student will apply spell check on the next book.

To the angel of angels who tells the best tourist tooth-brush story. If my mother were here she would be very proud to know someone of your strength, courage, and ability. You overcame every obstacle that has been thrown in your way; because of you, my road and the road of the agency now has a clear, unobstructed path.

To Beverly Pekala; when all was dark and appeared lost, there you were holding up the lantern of light, strength, and hope for not only myself, but for the countless victims that Project:Protect provides assistance to nationwide.

And finally, to my precious gift of love and joy, my child. It is for you that I have written this book. It is my hope that someday you understand that I wanted the world to be a better place.

preface

Defending Our Lives is intended to assist all domestic violence victims. It is my hope that the information introduced here will help guide women to achieve a healthier, safer life. We as a society can no longer allow women to lose their lives at the hands of those who profess to love them. In this country alone, eight to ten women lose their lives every day as a result of domestic violence. Domestic violence occurs every 14 seconds, 365 days a year.

How widespread is domestic violence? The U.S. Surgeon General has declared domestic violence as the nation's number one health problem. Physical abuse by their husbands or boyfriends is the single most common source of injury among women, more common than auto accidents, muggings, and rape by a stranger combined. Domestic violence is lethal. Every five years the number of women killed by relatives and acquaintances equals the number of American soldiers who died in the Vietnam War.

How many women must die? How many children must lose their innocence? How many more people must be emotionally scarred for life before we say enough is enough? How many movies will it take? How many victims must appear on talk shows before we deal head-on with this issue and treat domestic violence as a crime?

It will take more than public awareness or forcing police departments to act on their own or pressuring prosecutors to bring felony charges against offenders or appointing judges who will really listen to the evidence.

It will require enforcing laws to protect the victims. It will require effective treatment programs for offenders and treatment programs for victims. It will require the efforts of not just a few, but of all parts of our society. Not just the lawyers and judges, not just the lawmakers and social workers, not just the police organizations, but carpenters, plumbers, mail carriers, factory and office workers, care and insurance salespeople, doctors, nurses, community service organizations, churches and schools, and every segment of our society until we have put an end to the violence. As Abraham Lincoln said, "The strength of a nation lies in the homes of its people."

The sole intent of *Defending Our Lives* is to provide and inform the reader of the options available when violent abuse occurs in all relationships—whether the couple in question is married or simply dating, whether it is a heterosexual couple or a lesbian couple, whether the individuals involved are disabled. Any relationship that is violent is about power and control. No one is safe from this form of abuse and no one should be denied help because of prejudice. I am not a lawyer and cannot stress enough the importance of seeking your own legal counsel. Like our fingerprints, no two cases of abuse are the same.

—Susan Murphy-Milano, 1996

"my daddy's killing
my mommy"

THE BEST TIMES in our house were when my father would go away on hunting trips to Michigan or fishing trips to Canada. When he headed out with a bunch of other police officers to hunt deer in November, we all had a vacation. After he left, my mother would make plans for special outings with me and my younger brother, Bobby. I'd often wish that it was always just the three of us, and that there would be no more pain and suffering in our house. I became a clock watcher, counting down the remaining hours of peace, dreading the moment my father would walk back in the door.

I first remember seeing my father hurt my mother when I was about four. It was late at night and he was drunk. The sound of screaming and breaking glass woke me up. I ran into my parents' room and saw my mother with blood on her face. My father was smashing her head against the iron bed rail and yelling, "Why don't you listen to me? Why can't you ever do anything right?" Bobby and I stood in the bedroom door screaming and crying, holding on to each other while my father ordered us to stay away.

I looked at my mother to see what she wanted us to do. Her face was red and swollen, and she looked like she was badly hurt. "Go back, go back," she cried. "Mommy's okay, I'm okay." Reluctantly we went back to bed. A little while later I heard my mother scream, "He's gonna kill me, he's gonna kill me. Help me, somebody." I ran from my room to the kitchen, pulled a chair over to the phone on the wall, and dialed the operator. "Please, please," I cried. "My daddy's killing my mommy, come quick, please." Then I dropped the phone and ran back to hide in my bedroom. I hoped the lady on the other end could hear what was going on.

Finally, I heard the sirens and saw my father run out the front door. After checking on my mother, I went to the front window and peeked out through the curtains. I could see my father, in a white T-shirt and his blue police pants, talking to the other officers by the squad cars. One guy was scratching his head and another extended his hand to my dad. They seemed to be joking around. Then my father turned around and walked up the front steps to the house. My mother's blood was on his clothes. I ran and hid in my bed under the covers.

"You dirty bitch," he yelled at my mother. "You embarrassed me. No one embarrasses me." Then he started hitting her again.

For the next few days it was very somber around our house. Bobby and I quietly played with our toys, and my mother went to the doctor. My father was being very nice, not at all like the man who had been beating my mom. He said he was sorry, that he loved her, that he loved all of us. I was happy to hear his apology and felt relieved that nothing like that would ever happen again.

However, a few nights later I again awoke to the sound of my parents arguing. I looked over at Bobby, who was in his bed crying and shaking all over. I went and peeked out our bedroom door. My father's voice sounded so strange and I instantly knew he was drunk. He was accusing my mother of messing around with another policeman while he was at work.

"Bitch," he shouted. "You're a no-good nigger You're a lazy, worthless bitch." He sounded like he hated her. I didn't understand. He had said he loved her so much and that he would never hurt her again. But now I could hear him hitting her. I went into their room. She yelled at me, "Leave the bedroom, baby, get out." I screamed. She yelled again, "Go on, honey, go back to bed now." I ran to the kitchen, pulled the chair over, and again called the operator. This time I didn't say anything, I just let the phone hang there and ran back to Mommy.

The dresser mirror had been shattered and there was glass everywhere. I saw a gun. I couldn't tell who had the gun and who was trying to get it. Suddenly, the gun went off. I ran out of the bedroom, pulled the chain from the door, and, in my nightgown, ran out into the yard, screaming for help. I was hysterical, I didn't know who had been shot. Suddenly my father scooped me up and carried me back into the house, telling me to calm down. When he put me down, I ran to their room. I could smell the recently fired gun, but no one had been shot. "Everything is fine, baby," my mother said, pointing to the floor. "The bullet went into the floor near the heater. It's okay, no one got hurt. Mommy and Daddy were just arguing, but it's okay now." Then she took me back to my room. Bobby climbed in bed with me and my mother sat on the edge of the bed while we went back to sleep. We heard the front door slam. "It's okay," she said softly. "You know Mommy and Daddy love you very much. We would never do anything to hurt you. Sometimes Daddy gets angry, okay." She kissed us and we went back to sleep.

We didn't see our father for three days, and when he came home, he didn't say anything about what had happened. Our mother didn't talk about it either. But Bobby and I talked. Somehow in our minds we believed that if we picked up our room, didn't fight so much, and did as we were told, our parents would somehow stop fighting. We felt that we were to blame for what was happening.

My parents, Roberta Sharpe and Phillip Murphy, were married in September 1959 in Pope County, Illinois. A justice of the peace performed the ceremony when my mother was just seventeen years old and already pregnant with me. My father was twenty-four. They had met at Skip's Drive-in, a local hang-out in Melrose Park, Illinois. (Skip's Drive-in was the kind of place where guys met girls and won their hearts based on the kind of car they drove.)

My father reported to the police academy the morning

after they were married and he graduated in February 1960, two days before I was born. Within three months my mother was pregnant again, with my brother Bobby. As a rookie cop with the Chicago Police Department, my dad didn't earn much, so he took an extra job with the transit security so they could put away money for a home.

My mother was a happy teenager, soft-spoken but with a very hearty laugh. Even later in life, when she was often not very happy, her laugh stayed with her. She was short and looked even shorter next to my father, who was over six feet tall.

While my mother was warm and approachable, my father was impatient. He tended to snap at the smallest provocation. Dad was the strong, silent type, with striking features. He carried himself with confidence and had a presence that turned heads. Those who knew him described him as a "man's man" and a "cop's cop." He was the kind of man who would take a bullet for his partner. He held himself in reserve, studying other people, a serious man who didn't have much of sense of humor.

Most people thought of Dad as a wonderful provider, husband, and father. In his world, the fact that he was a cop and a strong Irish Catholic counted for a lot. The members of the police force judged you by your skin color, religion, and ethnic background, and my father won on all three counts.

In 1965 my father was promoted from patrolman to detective with the robbery division. I remember feeling proud of my father when I went to the police station with him. We walked in and everyone greeted him. They could tell I was his daughter and people came over to tell me I was pretty and lucky to have such a person for my daddy. The other police officers were his friends, the only friends I can ever remember him having. At times they appeared to mean more to him than his own family. Being a policeman was everything to my father, and his most prized possession was his tin shield. He never went anywhere without his badge or his gun.

Once on Grandma Caroline's birthday, the four of us went out with my grandmother to celebrate at our favorite Chinese restaurant. When we arrived, the twins who owned the place came over to my father and greeted him warmly and with obvious respect. After we'd eaten a nice dinner, my father asked for the check. The waiter told him that the meal was on the house. My father's face turned slightly red and he called one of the owners over to the table. The man proudly told us that just the week before, my father had caught the robber who had held him up at gunpoint. The money had even been returned. He told my father that he wanted to show his appreciation.

My father responded, "I'm off duty, and with my family having dinner here because you have the best food. What happened last week, that was work. That was what I get paid to do. Now I'm just a customer, so please give me the check."

For ten minutes my father argued with the owner. Finally, my father asked my mother to get his wallet from her purse and said he was going to leave the cost of the meal on the table, check or not. I asked him why he was paying the bill. He leaned over, looked at me, and said, "I am a policeman and I'm paid to catch bad people. That does not entitle me or us to a free meal. That's not how it works. You can't take something for nothing just because someone offers it to you. When you get older, you'll understand the importance of paying your own way."

I thought about that night for weeks and I never forgot it. I thought about how my dad did a dangerous job, catching bad men and taking them to jail. I started to notice other things he did that showed he was a policeman, like always taking a table where he could watch the door and see whoever was coming in or going out of the place.

Twenty years later, after my parents were dead, I ran into one of the restaurant owners at a political function. Because of the media attention I had been receiving, he knew who I was. He told me he remembered the night my father caught the men who held up his restaurant. "Your father was a great man," he told me. "No matter what he did, I will always remember him as a good man."

One night when I was nine years old and still wetting my bed, my mother woke me up as she always had done to change the sheets. Shortly after, we heard Dad's key in the front door. As my mother hurried to get the soiled sheets out of my room, she bumped into my father. "Wet the bed again, did she," he said. I could tell he was drunk by the sound of his voice. He and my mother began to argue. "Why do you give in and change the sheets. I've told you before, the only way she'll stop is to spend a whole night in her own mess. For God's sake, Roberta, she's nine years old." He was so angry, he slammed and locked their bedroom door. My brother came out to see what was going on. "Get back into bed," my father yelled. My parents were arguing, when I heard a crash of some kind. I got out of bed and found that my door was locked from the outside and I couldn't get out. The fighting lasted a long time. Without any interruption he beat Mom mercilessly.

When we woke up the following morning, Grandma Caroline was there and Mom was in the hospital. The next day my father picked us up and took us to the hospital, where, upon entering the hospital, he made a big display to the security guard, showing him his badge. When I saw Mom lying in the hospital bed, I felt sick. There was tape around her body, a brace on her knee, her face was all swollen, and she was wearing sunglasses. I asked her to take off the glasses, but she wouldn't.

I was boiling with anger. I was angry at God because I couldn't understand why he would let this happen. I knew from the prayers we said every night that there was a person in the sky who kept track of when you were good and when you were bad. If you didn't say your prayers or go to church, you could wind up in some bad place. But what was he punishing my mother for?

When my father left the room, my mother took off her sunglasses. Her eyes were very red, with little bloody lines in them. It looked like my father had hit her in the face with something very hard. She didn't look like my mom. We were there only a little while before my father came back. He whispered something in my mother's ear and kissed her on the forehead. For the next week Grandma Caroline took care of us and we didn't see our dad very much. The days and nights passed in kind of a fog—we marked the time by watching our favorite TV. Captain Kangaroo, Woody Woodpecker, and Casper the Ghost: These were the things that stayed the same, that made Bobby and me laugh. These cartoons and a bowl of Froot Loops kept us going each morning. When Mom finally came home, I felt like the earth had been set right again. Afterward, it seemed that my parents were fighting all the time.

Even when Christmas was coming, my father was the only one who even pretended to be merry. Late one Christmas Eve, Bobby and I were awakened by the sound of the screen door being ripped from its hinges. My father was smashed.

We heard him go into the kitchen, get a drink, then walk into the bedroom. He was trying to wake Mom up, telling her that he was hungry. "Phil, be quiet, be quiet, you'll wake the kids," she was saying. "This is Christmas morning. Please don't start."

Then his voice, mocking her: "What do you mean, don't start." He got louder. "I'll do what I fucking well please, do you hear me? If I want to get gasoline and pour it all over this house, my house, and light a match, there isn't a fucking thing you can do about it." I could hear my mother protesting, asking him to calm down, to be quiet. "Get off your goddamn ass and make me something to eat now," he said. I lay in my bed listening to her move around the kitchen.

When Bobby and I got up the next morning, we were eager to open our presents from Santa. Everything changed when we walked into the living room and saw Dad waiting there with a vodka bottle and a glass of ice. I took one look at him and tried to run back to bed. I didn't care about Christmas presents or about Santa Claus. But my father, barely able to speak much less keep his eyes open, insisted we open our presents in front of him. Mom came in and looked at us. Her eyes told us to do it and not say anything. I opened up presents and tried to act happy and merry, all the time wishing I could get away. We ate breakfast and, after my father passed out, my mother called our relatives and told them not to come over. My father didn't wake up until the next day.

Whenever my father was working long hours, things would be quiet. During these periods I wanted desperately to believe that life in our house would get better.

One year, as my tenth birthday approached, my mother and I planned a big party. The night before my party, I heard my father talking to my mother. I told myself it was okay; sometimes they would just talk. I braced myself, hoping he wouldn't kill her. All I knew was that the next day was my birthday and I didn't want anything to ruin it. When I heard his voice rise, I huddled down in my bed, holding my breath. He started swearing at my mother and I could hear her crying, asking him to be quiet.

His life would have been different, he said, if he hadn't married her.

"Well, divorce me," my mother said, "let me go."

"I'll see you rot in hell before I ever let that happen," he shouted. "If I want, I can burn you and the kids and the house all up, and just leave and no one will ever find me." He kept repeating himself, taunting her. "Where are you going? You've got nowhere to go. I'm not letting you go, do you hear me? I'll see you burn in hell first.

"Keep it up, Roberta. Who do you think people are gonna believe? Certainly not you. They'll throw you in the crazy house. 'Cause you're nuts, you need help. If I wanted to, I could make a phone call and have them take you away, no questions asked." I could hear him laughing.

That night I thought he would burn down the house right then and there. I was scared and confused. I thought about climbing out the bedroom window and running away. I realized that no one would help us. Hadn't he just said as much to my mother? I couldn't understand. Why was he doing this? Why were we being punished?

The next morning we followed Mom into the kitchen and watched her pour all the liquor down the sink, bottle after bottle. My father was passed out cold in the bedroom. Then she packed two suitcases and we put on our coats and walked down the street to the bus stop. We rode three buses to my grandmother's house. When we got there, my mom's mother just looked at us. Mom asked if we could stay, but my grandmother said there wasn't enough room.

"Go on, go back to Phil," she said. "It'll be all right."

Dragging our suitcases, we headed back out the door and into a movie theater to see *Peter Pan*. We sat through it twice until Mom looked at her watch and said it was time to go home. I hoped my father wouldn't be there when we arrived. I got my wish. He didn't come home for three days.

Looking back, I can see there was a definite rhythm to our lives. There were periods when all was relatively calm and "normal," then all hell would break loose and Mom would have to go to the doctor or to the hospital. Sometimes the police came to the house, but they always left without doing anything to help my mother. Then we'd return to "normal." I was always wary, even during the calm periods, because I knew that the yelling and the beatings would return.

If there had ever been a time when I thought I would wake up in a "normal" family, those days were over. My father was able to silence us all with his temper and his threats.

When he wasn't working, he was either hunting, fishing, or drinking. He usually left the house around the time I was getting home from school, and returned after a late night working on the streets and drinking at the tavern across the street from the station. Then he'd sleep until he had to go back and do it all over again. We had to tiptoe around when he was home. The shades and curtains of the house were always drawn. In the winter it was dark and gloomy and I would wake up and not even know if the sun was out.

Dad monitored all of our activities. If Bobby and I wanted to go outside and play, we would have to tell him that we were going to play hide-and-seek, or whatever, before he'd let us go.

It was even worse for my mother. When she decided she wanted to learn how to drive, he told her no, "You are not learning how to drive." Since their marriage she'd been forced to use a baby buggy or a little red wagon to bring groceries home. Now, with the closing of a nearby store, she'd have to walk two extra miles to get food and other necessities.

Because he refused to let her get a job, she poured all her energy into the PTA, happily organizing bake sales and fairs, and running parents' committees. One evening when I was in the fourth grade, my mother was heading out the door to a PTA meeting, when my father stopped her and told her she couldn't go. His voice was very forceful, the kind of voice I imagined him using with criminals. "You are not going anywhere this evening, I don't care where you have to be." She pleaded with him, reminding him that she was on the board and that she had to be there. "I'm going to take care of that," he shouted, pulling her into the bathroom and slamming her head against the porcelain bathtub. The next thing I knew he was putting us all in the car and we were driving to the hospital. Her head was in his lap and he was putting pressure to it with a towel to stop the bleeding. Bobby and I were in the backseat.

He warned my mother not to say a word to anybody. "You slipped and fell, right? Do you understand me? Am I making myself clear?" My mother was quiet. I started to ask him why he had done this, but he slammed on the brakes and turned around and looked at me. "I've told you once, I've told you twice. Little children should be seen and not heard. Am I making myself clear?"

I nodded my head yes.

■

One afternoon after school, my mother took me and Bobby out by the gangway and told us we were going to have a fire drill. We were supposed to call out her name when we came home from school, and if she didn't answer, we were not allowed to come in the house. We asked her why, and she explained that it was a game, an important game.

"We are going to play the game fair and square and you have to do what I ask you to do. If I don't answer, you are not to come in the house." From then on Bobby and I did as our mother asked, we never again entered the house without first calling her name and waiting for her to answer.

By the time I was ten Mom was getting sick and tired of living in constant fear. "This is no life for me and my kids," I overheard her say to someone on the telephone.

Then the next day, when Bobby and I returned home from school, our mother sat us down and told us that we were going away. To a place where we would be happy and not have to worry about Daddy coming home drunk and hurting Mommy or us. She wouldn't tell us where we were going, she only said we would be safe and that this was our little secret.

A couple of weeks later we took a cab downtown to the bus station. I was so thrilled by the way my mother was acting that it didn't matter where we were going or what toys I had to leave behind. I could feel how close we were to freedom and that was all that mattered. Boarding the bus, my heart felt heavy and my palms cold and sweaty. We were going, we were going, and we weren't coming back.

We hadn't been on the bus very long, when it stopped and the driver opened the door. My father got on. His face was beet red and his eyes looked possessed. He just motioned with his finger to my terrified mother, and we all got up and followed him off the bus. The driver went around the side of the bus and handed our suitcases to my father. My dad put us in an unmarked squad car and drove a hundred miles an hour back to the house.

He locked Bobby and me in our bedroom. We heard him drag my mother into their bedroom and hit her. We heard screams. It seemed to go on forever, then it suddenly stopped. We heard the front door slam shut. My father had left.

My mother opened the door to the bedroom, came in, and just sat on the floor crying. Her clothes were torn, her lip was swollen and bleeding, and her nose was bleeding. A big bruise was blossoming on her left eye and cheek. She called a cab and the three of us went to the hospital. A couple hours later my father picked us all up from the hospital and we drove in silence back to the house.

About three months later my mother told me she was pregnant. Mom was upset because she didn't think it was right to be bringing a little baby into our turbulent house. Although the word "rape" was not used, she told me that my father had forced himself on her and that he wanted her to be pregnant so she wouldn't leave.

I was very, very confused. How could anyone do this to someone he supposedly loved? Seeing my mother in such pain made me feel helpless. I thought what happened was my fault. If I hadn't been born, none of this would be happening. They got married only because of me. In my mind I had learned to take responsibility for everything that happened.

I wasn't sure I wanted a little brother or sister. My father wasn't hitting my mother as much, but his words were just as cruel as ever. I didn't even think of him as my dad anymore. When my mom went into labor in March 1971, all I felt was panic. We all jumped in the car to go to the hospital emergency room. As we waited for the nurses to take my mother upstairs, my parents were arguing again. She was begging my dad to sign some papers so she could get her tubes tied. Finally, he relented and said he would do it. After my little sister Patricia was born, it turned out he hadn't signed the papers after all. There I was, looking at my pretty little sister, and I still couldn't escape their arguing. My mother was crying.

"Phillip, why didn't you sign the papers? How could you do this to me?" He told her he didn't believe in it, it was against his religion. My mother responded that it was her body, her life, and it should be her choice. He shot back. "Obviously, that's why they require two signatures!"

"Oh, bullshit, Phillip, religion has nothing to do with it," she shouted back. When the doctor walked in, my father said we had to go, and we headed for home.

Grandma Caroline took care of us while Mom was in the hospital. I loved my grandmother, but I wondered if she understood what was happening in our house. I couldn't understand how such a warm, wonderful woman had raised such a terrible man.

When Mom came home with the baby, she seemed to have a new kind of strength. She said that since I was twelve she could confide in me. She told me that she had dreams of finishing her high school education, of learning how to drive and of getting a job. It was the only way she was getting out, she said. She told me she knew that my father had been controlling everything we did, but that she was going to stop that. She didn't know how yet, but she was going to do it. I believed her. Talking with her this way made the horror of our lives a little easier.

My father continued to come home angry, complaining that the baby cried too much, that nothing in the house was right, He would blow up at the slightest inconvenience—if his socks were not properly folded together, or if his shirts were not starched the way he wanted.

When he wasn't around, we'd curl up on the sofa together, watching old movies on TV, and my mother would quietly talk about her dreams and plans. I would lean against my mom with my head on her shoulder and dream with her. I felt she was the most beautiful and loving woman and I couldn't stand to see her hurt. I hated my father for relentlessly teasing her about her weight, for trying to beat her spirit down by telling her that no one would ever listen to her. "I wear a badge," he would remind her. "You wear an apron. Dummy up, Roberta. Dummy up. You're not as smart as me."

■

By the time I started high school, the relentless pattern of our lives still had not changed. My father walked through the house as if he were the perfect man who had been cursed with a wife who didn't recognize his perfection. He fought with us continually. I think he felt he commanded more respect from the perpetrators he arrested than he did from his own family. I promised myself that I was going to get out of there and then come back to get my mom out. Sometimes I sat with her, hoping that the doorbell would ring and a policeman would tell us that my father had been killed in the line of duty.

I didn't even feel guilty thinking this. How could I? It would be a release from living in fear of the next explosion. My father was a ticking time bomb when he drank. There were many nights when my brother and I were afraid to go to sleep. My father would be so drunk, it was as if he didn't know who we were, threatening to kill us all. Because when he drank he was not our dad, he was the enemy we all feared.

My mother had developed migraines as a direct result of having been hit in the head too often. When she finally consulted her doctor about them, she was told there was nothing to be done. Mom's doctor was a Holocaust survivor and seemed to empathize with her. At one point he showed me the numbers tattooed on his arm and told me that just as he had to live with the scar to remind him of his suffering, my mother would have to live with her scars.

"They can't be seen and no one has branded a number on her," he said. "But your mother has the same type of mark. It will probably never heal, but she's marked and owned."

The doctor was a gracious and generous dispenser of pills for my mother, and he would find medical reasons to put her in the hospital so she could get some rest.

She was also having other medical problems and was scheduled to have a hysterectomy. My father fought with her about the hysterectomy, telling her she couldn't leave the house and the kids for four weeks, but ultimately she went ahead with the operation. While she was away for the surgery, my father yelled at me that I wasn't doing things the way he needed them done, not starching and ironing his shirts properly. When I talked back to him, he smacked me in the face and I refused to talk to him for days.

For many years my mother had wanted to learn how to drive, and one day she finally worked up the nerve to sign up for lessons. We kept her secret and it was fun to see how giddy she was over sneaking off to the classes. My father found out about the lessons when the instructor called to cancel a class. He ranted and raved about it for days. He was also furious with Bobby and me because he knew that we were her allies. This time my mother didn't collapse under his tirade.

She waited for him to go away on one of his fishing trips with his buddies, then she finished the remaining lessons and passed the driving tests.

The day she got her driver's license she came home and danced around the kitchen like a schoolgirl. She then sat down, took a deep breath, and drew out a budget to figure out how much she would need to buy a car and get insurance. Bobby and I promised to keep it a secret. We kept all her dreams a secret. I think we sensed that her dreams helped her to cope with her situation. We didn't realize then that it would take three years for her to buy a car.

As my eighteenth birthday approached, I began making plans to move out. I found an apartment nearby in order to be close to my mother. As much as I hated being in the house, I still slept there a few nights a week. I fantasized about moving Mom in with me, of getting her away from my father. We children were greatly relieved when she somehow talked my father into letting her work during the hours Patricia was in school. She didn't tell me that she had been going to night school until after she received her high school diploma in 1979.

Once she graduated and was working, she filed for divorce. Despite all the cruelties my father had inflicted upon her, all she asked for in the divorce petition was minor maintenance to support my younger sister. (My brother had just enrolled at Southern Illinois University, so he was already out of the house.)

Still, she played it safe and waited to have the papers served while she and Patricia were on a trip to Florida, visiting old friends. I'm sure she felt safer being far away when he received the papers. I was working so hard and was so preoccupied with my own life that I didn't know she had filed until I rode over to the house to pick up some clothes I'd left there.

When I walked in I found my father sitting at the kitchen table in his underwear and T-shirt, crying uncontrollably. A sheriff had come by to deliver the summons. My father asked me if I would sit down. I was caught off guard by his request, by the plaintive tone in his voice. He asked me if I knew about the divorce papers, and I told him I didn't.

"Read this," he said, handing me the papers. "How could she say these things about me? Twenty years of marriage and I always gave her my paycheck. I always let her do what she wanted, and now she does this."

I didn't know what to say. He seemed so emotionally drained and confused. It was the only time I ever saw him break down.

"I love your mother," he pleaded. "I love every one of you children. What do I need to do to make things right?"

Even though he seemed quite pathetic, I saw that he had been cleaning his guns, two of which were lying on the table between us. I tried not to stare at the shiny metal, but felt terrified because I knew he was capable of exploding in an instant. I told him that I was late for work and started to leave, trying not to give him any reason to become angry. When I rose to leave, my hands were sweating and my knees were about to buckle from fear. I told myself, "Just put one foot in front of the other. Pick up your bike and slowly walk away."

That night I called my mother in Florida and told her that Dad had gotten the papers. "Don't come home for a while," I said. "Stay down there as long as you can."

She stayed in Florida and my father took a leave from work, went to Florida, and convinced her to reconcile with him. She told me he begged her to drop the suit, and when she refused, he threatened to kill her. He asked her how she'd feel leaving her children without a mother.

When my mother told me that my father had threatened her into reconciliation, I was furious, but I didn't know what to do. She calmed me down by telling me that she had pushed him to far. That she would stay with him and be more cautious. That her faith would protect her. With that rationale, she went back to her life with him. It hurt me to talk to her sometimes, because I could feel the pain behind the front she tried to put up. I worried about Patricia.

I talked to my mother almost every day, even after I married in 1982 and moved farther away. From time to time she reminded me of her plans to leave, but she kept putting them off, saying she would wait until Patricia graduated from high school. Mom enrolled in night school at a junior college to learn accounting, but that didn't completely satisfy her. Sometimes I felt as though she were living vicariously through me. She was proud of the work I was doing at a large brokerage firm and was thrilled to hear about my work.

I didn't share my success with my father, who was growing angrier as he aged. His drinking was now totally out of control. Patricia came to stay with me and my husband, Les, on long weekends. She often asked me what I thought would happen. We were always waiting for the bomb to go off.

When Les and I decided to take a Christmas cruise in 1985, I laughed with my mother and told her to send a telegram if anything exciting happened. Otherwise, I told her, "I'll see you in a week."

Two days into the cruise, as we headed for the island of St. Croix, they called my name over the loudspeaker. I couldn't imagine why anyone was paging me while I was on vacation.

A telex had arrived for me. It said, "Call home or your office immediately. Medical emergency. It's your father. Love, Mom."

At that moment my stomach was doing somersaults. I felt as though my heart had been placed in my hand and it was beating uncontrollably. I didn't know what had happened, so I began to imagine the worst. I thought, this is it. He's dead. He's been shot in some heroic fashion and he's dead. Or there's been a serious accident and his gun went off. Whatever it was, I knew it was serious.

I tried calling the house, but no one was there, so I called my office. "Where the hell are you, Susan? We've been trying to reach you. Do you realize we sent a telegram to every ship at sea trying to track you down."

When my business partner, Robert, calmed down, he explained that my father was in critical condition. He had suffered a severe stroke and wasn't expected to live. I asked him to call my mother and tell her he had located me.

For a moment I was in shock. Les asked me what I wanted to do. I didn't know . . . then, all of a sudden, I felt a big weight lift from my shoulders as I began to think about the long-awaited peace my mother would finally have.

"Nothing," I said. "We're going to finish the cruise. We'll try calling my mother later."

At dinner that evening the news had spread throughout the ship. Everyone was trying to console me. "If they only knew," I thought to myself.

Later that evening we went back to the ship's office and I was able to reach my mother.

She said we shouldn't return home, but should try to enjoy ourselves. Whatever happened, she would delay any arrangements until we returned.

As it turned out, there was no way for us to leave the ship, so we enjoyed the remainder of our vacation. We returned Chicago on New Year's Eve and I called my mother, expecting her to tell me when the funeral would be held. Instead, she told me Dad was still in the hospital. My father had tubes and machines all around him. His hands and legs were tied to the bed and he was in a coma. When I asked why he was tied up, the nurse said he had been trying to pull the tubes out. Just then a nun walked into the room, carrying rosary beads in one hand and a Bible in the other.

"Still no change," she said. "I'll continue to pray." As she walked out, she touched my shoulder.

A few days later my father's condition improved. When I saw him again his body was in the fetal position. With the bed rails up, he looked like a helpless child in a grown man's body. The sight of him made me feel sad and guilty for wishing him dead. The doctors weren't sure if he would ever fully recover. He had lost his speech and was paralyzed on his right side and partially paralyzed on his left. His mouth curved up toward his nose.

My father had awakened my mother in the middle of the night, pleading for help. She at first thought he was drunk. Later in the emergency room, a doctor asked her if my father was on any medication or if he was an alcoholic, because their efforts to revive him weren't taking effect. My mother said he just looked at him and shook her head, no. As the doctor was leaving, Patricia ran up to him and told him that yes, my father drinks a lot and takes a lot of Valium. Patricia subsequently regretted having provided the information that saved his life.

My father didn't die, but his recovery took a very long time. He couldn't speak or walk. He couldn't really do anything for himself. His right side was particularly paralyzed, but he was determined to get back to normal. He was in the hospital for more than a year. During his hospitalization my mother had the freedom to do as she wished, including buying the car she had wanted for so long. She also found a better job.

After two years my father was essentially better, with only lingering paralysis in his right hand and leg. He was home on medical disability, waiting to retire from the police force, when he turned.

Dad began calling Mom at her work constantly, asking her what she was doing, when she was coming home. Some days he'd call thirty or forty times with trivial questions like what she was bringing home for dinner. He was suspicious of how she spent her time, accusing her of having affairs with both male and female coworkers.

Mom was now biding her time, waiting for the right moment to leave. I began having daily conversations with her about when she would leave. She didn't want to leave until my sister had graduated from high school. She decided she could deal with the verbal abuse. At first she said it was easier than getting beaten because it was only words. However, my father had started drinking again, and although he wasn't able to be as physically violent as he had been in the past, his verbal abuse of my mother increased to the point where she had no peace.

He also began to obsess about where my mother was at all hours of the day. He would park his car outside her office, watching to see when she left. One day my father had come up behind her when she was walking into the house and told her that the next time she was late he would shoot her.

I told her that she had to leave even though Patricia still had a year of high school left. She had to get on with her life. A few weeks later I went apartment hunting with her.

We found an apartment in the same neighborhood so my sister wouldn't have to switch schools. My mom said she wanted to move and get settled into her new apartment before she filed for divorce.

About a week later, while my mother was at work, she was served with divorce papers. My father claimed irreconcilable differences and mental cruelty. I think he wanted to make himself look like the victim, a dependent person abandoned by my mother. Family friends told me that he was telling everyone that she suddenly left him all by himself.

Although he had filed for divorce, he continued to stalk her, monitoring her every move. He stopped by her apartment constantly, ringing the buzzer at various hours of the night to see if someone would let him in. He called around the clock, hanging up when someone answered the phone. He continued to harass her at work.

To save money, they had one attorney representing both of them. My mother tried to explain to their lawyer that my father wasn't all he appeared to be, that he was very manipulative. The attorney was the son of a former policeman, a friend of my father's. She wanted him to know that he shouldn't believe my father. But Mom said she could tell from the expression on his face that he didn't believe her.

My parents' divorce was finalized in March 1988. My mother was ecstatic but my father wasn't satisfied. He was angry with everyone, including me, for helping her move out and get on with her life. My father's fifty-fifth birthday/retirement was exactly one year away, so for tax purposes my parents decided to wait until then to sell the house. Dad continued to call Mom and to stalk her. She ran into him at the bank or the store too many times for it to be a coincidence. Patricia and I wanted her to stay away from him and not go to the house by herself, but my mother seemed undaunted.

Mom had lost some weight and was taking care of herself, enjoying simple pleasures like having her hair done. She talked about using the money she'd get from the sale of the house to move to Florida, where my sister was now in college.

In the meantime, we planned a grand Christmas holiday, our first where we wouldn't have to deal with Dad. We rang in the New Year at a gala event downtown. After New Year's I noticed my father was hanging around the apartment parking lot more and more. I warned my mother to be extra careful and especially not to go to the house alone, not even to sign the papers for the sale of the house. I promised her I'd find somebody to handle it, or I would take care of it myself.

"Whatever you do," I said, "don't go meet him by yourself."

On January 17, 1989, I called Mom and we made plans for the upcoming weekend. Something didn't feel right, so later that night I decided to stop by for a visit. She wasn't home and so I let myself in. It looked like she would be right back, because the lights were on and a box of her favorite pastries was on the table, unopened. I hung around for a while. Eventually I left her a note and went home.

The next morning I called her at home and at work. A coworker told me she wasn't in. Because my mother was in customer service, she was often busy with calls or in the warehouse checking on something. So I thought she was just away from her desk. I got busy with my own work, and by the time I called back, everyone had left for the day.

That night after I got home I called her answering machine and picked up her messages. From the messages I discovered no one knew where she was. There were messages from her office, from my grandmother, and from some of her friends. At that point I panicked and immediately drove to her apartment. I could tell she hadn't been there since I had left the night before. The lights were still on and my note hadn't been removed from the refrigerator. I looked around and then ran out to my car and drove in a daze to the house I had grown up in.

Mom's car was parked out front. I couldn't imagine why she was there, but I knew something was very wrong.

It was two or three in the morning and the lights were on in the house. I left my car in the middle of the street and ran to the front door. I rang the bell, but there was no answer. I went around to the side of the house and knocked. No response. I climbed up onto the air conditioner at the back of the house and pounded on the storm window. Inside, the television was on with the volume up high. I called to them to open the door.

The next-door neighbor came out and asked if I wanted to use the phone, but I told her to go back inside and I'd call out if I needed her. I walked to the back door.

The glass window was broken out and had been boarded with a piece of heavy wood secured by nails. I tried to push the board in so I could unchain the door and gain entrance. With the back of my elbow I continued to push hard on the wood, so hard that I was sweating. Finally, I was able to pry away a nail or two and reached in and unchained the door.

As I stepped up on the base of the landing, I could see a body on the kitchen floor. I didn't know who it was, but the stench was so overpowering that I turned and ran out of the house to escape the smell. I don't remember how long I was in the house, or if I ever made it up the four steps from the landing to the kitchen. My memory of that night is still foggy. I ran to the neighbor's house and pounded on the door, asking to use the telephone. I dialed 911. When the operator asked how I knew there was a body on the floor, I hung up and called my father's old unit.

The first thing out of my mouth was "Officer down, this is Phil Murphy's daughter." I knew that those inside-the-corps words would generate an immediate response. When I was asked to repeat myself, I responded, "There is a body in the house. I don't know whose, but there is a body."

"Where's your father?" he asked.

"I don't know. Please send somebody."

"All right. Where are you? Can you meet the police?"

"Yes," I replied. "I'm just next door." I gave them the address and within a few minutes a dozen or more police cars were on the scene, lined up and down the street. There were also fire trucks, an ambulance, and paddy wagons.

I brought the officers down the gangway and directed them to the back of the house, where a fireman opened the back side door. In a flash I remembered my mother's fire drills. Here in the gangway we had played that odd game some twenty years earlier. I recalled my mother telling us not to come in the house if she didn't answer.

"Go and get help," she had said. At that moment I knew she was gone. Then the police went into the house. I wanted to go with them, but they wouldn't let me.

"That's my mother in there," I shouted. "I have a right to be with her. I'm not going. Leave me alone."

It took three police officers to get me into the house next door. One officer stayed with me, talking to me calmly and preventing me from leaving. A fireman came in to tell me that the door to the back of the bedroom was locked. He asked my permission to break the door in. I told him to go ahead. When he returned he gave the police officer a knowing look.

I pleaded to be let into the house, but was told to wait next door. I asked, "Is she . . . ? My parents, are they . . . ?" I couldn't say the words. The policeman just nodded his head yes. I had always tried to take care of my sister, but now there was nothing I could do to ease the pain. With trembling fingers I dialed my sister's number in Florida and gave her the news. I could feel myself going numb; my whole world had collapsed.

About half an hour later, a police chaplain arrived. He asked what denomination my parents were. He was a Catholic priest and wanted permission to perform last rites. I nodded yes.

A detective came to tell me that he had to take some information and that he was very sorry for what had happened. He said he knew both my parents, that he had worked with my dad for years, that my dad was a wonderful man. He was sorry for the loss. After the detective finished questioning me, the priest returned.

"They're getting ready to carry your parents out of the house now. You'd better stay inside," he said.

With that I grabbed my coat and headed for the neighbor's porch. I was appalled. "Why are they carrying my parents' bodies to that disgusting paddy wagon? Where's the ambulance?"

The priest who was directly behind me said, "The ambulance has left and sometimes bodies are carried in the paddy wagon."

"That's disgraceful!" I blurted out. I wanted to run over as the bodies were carried out one by one. Two police officers stationed themselves at the bottom of the neighbor's steps.

By now it was daylight, and the house was clearing out. When everyone had left I was able to go back in the house. I walked around the house, stunned. I sat in my father's favorite chair in the living room. An empty carton of orange juice and half-gallon bottle of vodka were on a tray table beside the chair. On the floor was an ashtray spilling over with very short cigarette butts.

Reaching under the chair, I found a loaded gun and my

father's wallet. Inside the wallet was a note dated January 17, 1989. There was no signature, but it was his handwriting. It said, *To whom this may concern. This is business only. I did what I had to do. No one leaves me and gets away with it, so I'm taking care of business.*

Later that evening I met with my father's ex-partner and he explained how my parents died. My father had shot my mother in the back of the head at close range. She died in the kitchen. Then he had gone into the bedroom and locked the door. He sat there drinking for a while, then put the gun to his head and killed himself.

Over the next few months I found many more pieces of paper written in his hand, with dates and times on them, detailing what my mother was doing and where she was at various times during any given day. He even kept records of their phone, taping some of the conversations. He was obsessed with her and wrote about how he couldn't live without her.

At the time this tragedy happened, I believed that no one else had gone through what I was going through, that this was a one-in-a-million case.

I was wrong.

recognizing domestic violence

AFTER MY MOTHER was killed by my father, I felt completely helpless and absolutely furious. I knew that my mother's murder could have been, and should have been, prevented. I wanted to do something. To assuage my grief and fury over my mother's death, I decided to become involved in helping other women who have been repeatedly battered by those who profess to "love" them. I formed Project:Protect to empower women across the country who are victims of violent abuse in their own homes.

I was stunned by the numbers. I discovered that wife abuse is the most common but least reported crime in the U.S. According to FBI statistics, a woman is beaten every 15 seconds and a rape is committed every 6 minutes. One in every eight women has, by the age of eighteen, been physically abused by a boyfriend, and half of all couples have had at least one violent incident. In the United States of America, bastion of democracy and proponent of individual liberty, more than two million women a year are severely beaten in their homes, and yet little attention is paid to them.

According to the Department of Justice, nearly half of all women murdered in this country are killed by their partners. According to the July 4, 1994, issue of *U.S. News and World Report,* this means 1,400 to 2,500 women are being killed every year. Not included in this figure are the countless number of women whose general health deteriorates in an abusive environment and whose lives are shortened because of the stress of continual beatings. Women who are habitually beaten have learned from painful experience that to fight back can incite more rage.

I am not being sexist in putting the emphasis on women as the victims of domestic violence. According to the U.S. Attorney General's office at least 94 percent of all cases of partner violence involve a man beating a woman.

In the years that I have been working with women who are abused by men, I have observed several things. Violence in the home usually escalates, becoming more frequent and severe over time. The first incident may be a shouting match which eventually, and for no apparent reason, leads to a slap. You are stunned. You can't believe he hit you. He apologizes and says "I'll never do it again, I love you." The two of you kiss and make up. A few weeks or months pass and everything appears to be fine. One day an argument starts over something foolish. This time he begins hitting you and/or throwing you around the room. You now need to realize that your relationship is in serious trouble. His unpredictable behavior could become life-threatening. You may be confused as to why anyone whom you love, and who loves you, would use physical force. You may think that you did something that warrants this kind of behavior. You need to recognize that this is domestic violence and that it's a crime. You need to take responsibility for your situation. Consider calling a domestic violence agency in your area for resources or advice.

If he hits you, it is a criminal act and you have the right to call the police for assistance. Let's say a complete stranger walked up to you and punched you in the nose, you would contact the police and have the person arrested. You would then go down to the police station, press charges, and finally go to court, to deter this individual from assaulting someone else. You should behave in the same manner toward an abusive partner. The person you are involved with doesn't go around hurting his coworkers, friends, or strangers, does he? Then why is it acceptable that he do this to you? Either he believes that he has the right to abuse you or he believes there will be no repercussions for his abusive behavior. That's why it's important to realize that you must take responsibility for protecting yourself.

WHAT IS DOMESTIC VIOLENCE?

Domestic violence is emotional or physical abuse, or the threat of physical abuse, between family or members including:

- Spouses
- Former spouses

- Parents
- Children
- Stepchildren
- Other persons related by blood
- In-laws from a current or previous marriage
- Persons who live together
- Persons who are dating or have dated or been engaged
- Persons who have disabilities and their caregivers

WHAT IS CONSIDERED
PHYSICAL ABUSE?

Physical abuse can include:

- Slapping
- Pushing or poking
- Kicking
- The twisting of any limbs
- Pulling hair
- Biting
- Choking
- Shaking or throwing someone around a room

- Any form of restraint
- Rape, i.e., forcing someone to have unwanted sex

Physical violence includes the use of:

- Guns
- Knives
- Blunt instruments
- Any other weapon

WHAT IS EMOTIONAL OR PSYCHOLOGICAL ABUSE?

Emotional or psychological abuse can take on many forms and patterns. The sole purpose of the abuser's actions is to dominate, manipulate, and control another person. The abuser can act out in the following ways:

- Name-calling or yelling
- Using of angry expressions or gestures
- Humiliation, either in public or private
- Isolation of the victim from family and friends
- Accusations of infidelity
- Constant belittlement of another person

- Constant questioning of the other person's judgment or decision-making abilities
- Threatening to leave
- Threats to take the children away forever
- Accusations of insanity
- Ignoring or minimizing the other person's feelings

The abuser will often keep close tabs on every penny you spend, giving you less than you need to buy groceries, keeping track of the mileage on the car, not allowing you or the children to seek needed medical attention, withholding medication, failing to assist with child care or housework.

THE WARNING SIGNS OF COMING ABUSE

- An increased use of alcohol or drugs
- A desire to have sex for the wrong reasons
- Insistence that you do things his way
- Clinging to you constantly
- Drawing you away from seeing family or friends
- Threats to commit suicide if you ever leave him
- Unpredictable behavior

ANNA AND PETER

Anna was twenty-one years old when she met Peter. "I was fortunate enough to grow up in a home where there was no violence. I had a very normal upbringing, a Lutheran education, and yet I still fell into this trap."

At first Anna thought that Peter just needed a friend, someone to do things and pal around with. "He had no one that he could talk with, and so I was there for him." Before Anna knew it, Peter was always around and clinging to her. He became extremely possessive and controlling. After they had been together for three months, he began to insist they marry and start a family. Being young and naive, Anna didn't realize what his threats meant until it was too late.

By a year into their marriage, and after they had their first child, Anna felt smothered, alone, and in fear for her life and that of her child. Peter's threats of harm if she didn't do what he asked of her were escalating and becoming more violent. Anna lost confidence in her ability to function as a person. At some point she remembers Peter threatening to "kill her if she ever left." And if he couldn't find her, he threatened to kill her family one by one until he found her. Anna believed she was trapped.

She felt helpless, and thought neither her family nor her friends could help her, so she didn't talk to anyone about her problems. Keeping Peter happy was Anna's daily challenge. He used the fact that she was deathly afraid of him against her. It was very difficult for Anna to live with a man who hated her enough to tell her that it would be nothing for him to kill her anytime he wished. When he told her she was a bad mother who didn't care about her child, she had to swallow her pride and resist answering back. When he told her that he didn't want her family around, she would agree. When he forgot to pick her up from the store or from work, she kept her anger inside. Anna blamed herself for being naive, for not recognizing what kind of man Peter really was. He was extremely unpredictable, loving her one day and hating her the next, blaming her for everything that went wrong in his life.

One day Anna lost her job. She had been the primary breadwinner of the family. When she found a new job, she discovered that her new company had a program for women in abusive relationships. She was hesitant about coming forward and asking for help. But after eight years of living with this man, she decided to see what they could do for her. She learned that it wasn't going to be easy, that the company would provide only so much assistance and that she was expected to take responsibility to do the rest. They made arrangements for her and her child to be transferred to another location. They directed her to housing, counseling, and divorce services. Today she has been away from Peter for almost four years. She is still with the same company and spending her spare time volunteering at a battered women's shelter, where she offers support and encouragement to others just like her.

Anna didn't see the warning signs or behavior patterns until she was already married to Peter. Domestic violence is a combination of threats, control, insults, and insane jealousy. The abuser attempts to isolate and overpower "his" woman. Certain behaviors can foreshadow coming violence.

In the July 4, 1994, issue of *Newsweek,* psychologist Amy Holzworth-Munroe says that abusers come in three categories. First, those men who hit their wives infrequently and are sorry for it. Second, those who are intensely jealous and fear abandonment. (The men in both of these groups are emotionally dependent upon their wives/partners and feel the need to control them.) Third, and the most dangerous, are men with antisocial personality disorder. Neil S. Jacobson, a marital therapist at the University of Washington, says that such men are "just like criminals who beat up everybody else when they're not getting what they want. Men who batter share something else: They deny what they've done, minimize their attacks, and always blame the victims." Lenore Walker, director of the Domestic Violence Institute in Denver, describes abusers as being "like Jekyll and Hyde—wonderful one minute, dark and terrifying the next."

In my work with victims of abuse, I've had no experience with batterers whose violence is infrequent and doesn't escalate. In most cases, as in the example of Peter and Anna, a batterer needs to be in total control of his wife/partner. He normally shifts between demonstrations of affection and intense abuse. Writing letters and keeping journals and written records are also characteristic of violent offenders. These writings often begin with remarks of love and pleas for their victim to return to them, and then build up with threats of bodily harm or death.

These threats must be taken seriously.

WARNING SIGNS

Men who become obsessed with or stalk someone they have been involved with often share similar characteristics. There are certain warning signs to watch out for.

- Extreme jealousy and possessiveness
- The need to control others
- Name-calling and use of derogatory remarks and/or constant put-downs
- Attempts to keep another person in isolation, away from family and friends
- Cruelty to animals
- Poor communication and coping skills
- Addiction to drugs and/or alcohol
- An antifemale attitude
- Tendency to blame others for their faults/mistakes
- A belief in male superiority
- A family history of domestic violence in adult life or childhood
- A self-righteous attitude

KENNETH AND ANGIE

Kenneth and Angie met at work. Because they lived in a small town in Arkansas, they often ran into each other at the store, church, or local hangout. They began dating and were married within a year. Like most violent offenders, Kenneth felt the need to control Angie. He was jealous of his new wife and questioned her constantly, especially when she returned home from work or the store later than he expected. Shortly after they were married, Kenneth began to beat Angie. Four months into their marriage he broke Angie's arm and nose.

Angie did everything right. She moved out of their apartment and obtained an order of protection from the courts. She also began saving money for a divorce.

From the day Angie left, Kenneth found ways to send notes and letters to her. Sometimes he put them on her windshield or slipped them under her apartment door. In his letters he told her that if she knew what was good for her, she would come back to him. God had joined them together in holy marriage and they would be together until death.

Dear Angie,

I really do love you with all my heart and soul. I know it seems as if all I do is upset you, that is not my intention. I am really hurting, as I am back and back to stay. I am also trying to make all the changes you want of me, and, love, I will make them! I just need to know you want me. I wish they could happen over-night but I know they will take time. Honey, I am really trying my best, and giving my all to you, us, and our marriage. That is what means the WORLD TO ME!! I am just really frustrated that you have not yet tried to put forth the same needed effort to me, us, and OUR MARRIAGE. I don't know, I can't read your mind! Choosing your independence, acting single, friends, relatives, etc. etc. over me, us, OUR MAR-RIAGE. Babe, that hurts, that hurts a lot! I want to give my all and do my best. Now and forever to you, to us, and OUR MARRIAGE. Don't you understand, don't you care? Honey, I am trying harder than I ever tried anything before in my life.

Over the course of eleven months Kenneth sent Angie one or two letters every day. All of his letters were signed "Love always forever and forever, your husband." And he usually added a P.S. like the one below.

I know I fucked up our marriage, but NOTHING, that LOVE, understanding, and all effort cannot correct! We both made mistakes, so please, let's start correcting those mistakes together, and together make our marriage GREAT. Now and forever if you really love me, and your love is true. YOU will find it in your heart to forgive me and start over one last time (no

more will ever be needed) TOGETHER WITH ME
NOW.

Kenneth's letters show how desperate he was and how
sorry he was for hurting her. He claims that he is willing to do
anything for just one more chance with Angie. Be forewarned,
a person does not alter his violent behaviors by simply waving a
magic wand. Kenneth clearly needs help. There are treatment
services available in many states for abusers such as Kenneth.
Most of them are listed in the yellow pages.

This letter is like so many written to victims of abuse who
have left their abusers. If you receive letters, tapes, or videos,
keep them in a safe place. They can be instrumental in obtaining an order of protection or in filing additional charges
against your abuser. This is a form of contact and in many
cases abusers can be prohibited by court order from writing,
calling, sending flowers and telegrams, etc.

FRED AND MARIE

Marie and Fred were engaged and planning to be married
in two months, when Marie's father became critically ill.
Marie's parents were divorced and Marie was her father's only
child, so she put her life on hold to care for him, postponing
the wedding indefinitely.

Marie, an executive with a major pharmaceutical company, said that Fred was romantic, sensitive, and attentive. He

was always there for her. He would bring her flowers for no reason. She found his presence very comforting when she was down. It was clear that Marie was the most important person in Fred's life and Marie loved being able to depend on him.

In May Marie's father died and she was devastated. Even Fred couldn't console her. In an effort to comfort Marie, Fred suggested that they get married right away. Marie, however, didn't want to get married, and for the first time Fred yelled at her. Marie was shocked, but Fred apologized immediately.

Several days later, when Marie still wouldn't set a new wedding date, Fred snapped. They had a loud, ugly argument and Fred slapped Marie hard across the face. Marie was stunned. She ordered Fred out of her house and has refused to reconcile with him despite his pleas for forgiveness and his promises never to hit her again.

Marie shared this story with me months later. During our discussion of Fred and his background, I told Marie that she had been very smart not to accept Fred's profuse apologies. His violence would no doubt have escalated if they had married. Fred's family background made him a prime suspect for domestic violence.

Fred had told Marie that his father, Bill, abused his wife and his six children both verbally and physically. Fred, the oldest boy, was a sensitive child whom the father called a sissy. To toughen Fred up, Bill was especially brutal to him. He slapped, punched, and kicked him for the smallest infraction. If Fred didn't respond quickly enough to a question about his schoolwork, Bill knocked him down.

Bill also slapped his wife, Ginger, for not moving quickly

enough when he called her. He beat her regularly, often for not keeping the house and the children as clean as he thought they should be.

Fred despised his father, but he also admired his "power" and desperately wanted his approval. Fred, in an effort to show his father that he deserved his approval, followed in his dad's footsteps and became a physician. Bill was unimpressed and continued to treat his adult son with disdain. Fred, in turn, had little respect for either of his parents, and was particularly contemptuous of his mother.

Marie described Ginger as having the lowest self-esteem of any person that she had ever met. All of the children appeared to disregard their mother, while Ginger, on the other hand, appeared grateful just to be in their presence. Marie had thought that marrying into a large family would be wonderful, but discovered being around Fred's family made her very uncomfortable.

Marie was right to be uncomfortable. Growing up in a family where violence was a common occurrence and in which the mother was treated as if she didn't matter set the stage for Fred to become a wife batterer. Marie said her biggest concern was that she and Fred had planned to have children. Marie couldn't imagine exposing her children to the kind of brutal environment that Fred had described from his childhood. It was this fear of replicating the domestic violence in Fred's family that led Marie to end the relationship the very first time he hit her.

It was the smartest thing Marie could have done. Far too often when women allow men to talk them into overlooking "one little" act of violence, whether verbal or physical, the next transgression is even more heinous. There are no "little" acts of abuse. Each violent act has the potential to lead to another.

A wealthy and prominent Chicago lawyer who hit his wife "only a few times" and twisted her arm once, eventually conspired to have her killed. Following the usual pattern, the lawyer was very controlling and demanded obedience from his wife. The wife, who had habitually been compliant, refused to accept his unfair settlement offer in a divorce he initiated. True to form, he was furious at not getting his way and responded by hiring someone to kill her. The husband's scheme was unsuccessful partially because the wife followed advice she had received to be extremely cautious. Although the husband has been convicted and sentenced to prison, the wife wisely remains wary that he may still try to harm her.

CHOOSING A SAFE RELATIONSHIP AND KNOWING WHEN TO BE CAUTIOUS!

Let's begin at the beginning. When you are first introduced to someone who sparks your interest, there are fireworks and butterflies in your stomach. As soon as you return home from a date, you call all your friends to let them know what a wonderful evening you had. You feel as though you're floating on air.

STOP! RED FLAG! WARNING . . . WARNING!

Your radar should automatically go off. You just met this person. The only thing you know about him is that he's handsome, sexy, and knows where to take a woman on a date. Having all these feelings is nice, but what do you actually know about this person? Did you check him out prior to agreeing to your date? This is usually a very vulnerable time. That automatic "love pilot button" goes into full gear and you are off like a horse at the starting gate.

Ask the person who introduced you to him the following questions:

- How well do you know him?
- How long have you known him?
- What does he do for a living?
- Do you know his family?
- Do you know where he grew up?
- Does he like to drink or do drugs?
- What are his hobbies?

No matter what they tell you, do your own research. In this society we are very careful about everything else that affects our daily lives, but we eagerly enter into relationships with people about whom we know next to nothing!

Begin by asking this person, before the first date or immediately after your first date, these questions in a nonthreatening manner:

- Where did he go to school?

- Where do his parents live?

- Are they still married?

- Was there violence in his home while he was growing up?

- If his parents are divorced, ask for a general reason.

- Did he have a happy, loving childhood?

- What type of relationship does he have with his parents?

- What kind of environment was he raised in?

- Has he ever been in trouble with the law? If so, for what?

- Has he ever been married?

- If he is divorced, why did the marriage end?

In addition to asking questions, observe how he handles his feelings. Does he express them easily? Does he seem mysterious? Is he using direct eye contact when answering your questions? Does he explain his unexpected presence by saying "I'm lonely"? "I missed you and couldn't bear to end my night without seeing your lovely face"? Does he invite himself to join you when you're going out with friends? In other words, is he invading all your free time?

In addition to the usual caution you should exercise when dating someone who drinks too much or uses drugs, you should be aware of characteristics potential abusers share. If he gets jealous when others admire, compliment, or take up your time or spends an unusual amount of money on you each time you get together, be careful. If he criticizes you for not always wanting to do what he wants or plans evenings without asking for your input, be wary. If he regularly calls you the minute you walk in the door or the moment he gets home, that's a warning sign.

Before you become involved in a serious relationship, check out his personal history and references. Obtain his:

- Full given name at birth

- Date of birth

- Social security number

- Address

Or just get a copy of his driver's license, it has all this information. Run a check on his license plate number. If he's been divorced, find out why, when, and where. Don't take his word for the reasons the marriage ended. Go to the courthouse in the county where he was divorced and obtain a copy of his file. If you are unable to get a copy made, review the file and take notes. Read everything in the records very carefully. This information is in the public record, so you are within your rights to ask for it. If he objects and gets angry about providing any of this information, something is wrong. There may be something he doesn't want you to know about. You need to tell him that you are doing this only for your own safety and peace of mind. If you don't have a way to check out his personal history, send Project:Protect a written request with the person's full name, his birth date, social security number, and address along with $50 and we'll run a check for you. Be sure to include a telephone number where you can be reached and a return address. (This service is available only in the United States.)

Just as I hope you practice safe sex, learn to practice safe relationships. Listen carefully to what he is actually saying rather than hearing just what you want to hear. We all want and need to be admired and made to feel special and loved, but it's essential that we learn to distinguish between caring love and obsessive control. Don't be like the horse at the racetrack ready to explode out of the gate at the start of the race. That horse is wearing blinders and sees only what's directly in front of him and nothing else.

■

calling the police

WHEN A VICTIM OF ABUSE calls the police for assistance, the police department is required to treat the situation as a crime. However, given that domestic violence is often not seen as a crime, when a woman calls the police for help the officer who responds can often behave as if he is not taking the woman's complaint seriously. The officer is responding to offenses committed between family or household members. It's not as though an officer has had to go out and match a description of someone you don't know who has just committed a crime. The abuse is between parties who know each other. That's why it's so important to know your rights as a crime victim. All too often the legal system can victimize you further because you don't know when to speak up or what your rights are.

As a victim you have the right to:

- Request that the responding officer assist you in providing for your safety and that of your children by escorting you to a friend's or relative's home, motel, or shelter.
- Insist the responding officer make out a report.
- Demand the officer take your statement.
- Insist the officer arrange for medical care for you or your child(ren) if such care is needed.
- Preserve the evidence of the crime.
- Arrest the offender.

You must also think about how you are going to respond when the police arrive at your home. There are several pointers you should follow:

- Stay as calm as possible. This may be hard to do, but the police need to understand you when you are placing your call for help and responding to their questions.
- You need to describe the incident with as much detail as possible: Remember you are the best witness to what has just occurred. The officer will take your statement by writing down your description of what happened. Then you should be asked to proofread what the officer has just written in order to make sure the information is correct. If you are not satisfied with the statement the officer has prepared, you have the right to have it changed.

- If you have sustained any bruises, marks, or cuts, or if property, such as your car or home has been damaged, show the responding officer, who will then document it because it's visible proof.
- If you have an order of protection, show the officer your documentation.
- Be sure to obtain your case or incident number before the officer leaves. This number allows you to follow up with your case.

If the responding officer refuses to assist you, telephone the police department and ask to speak with someone in charge. Calmly explain the situation and be sure to write down the name of the person you speak with. If the officer becomes threatening to you in any way, you can file a complaint against that officer through the department's Internal Affairs Unit.

WHAT HAPPENS TO THE ABUSER?

In order for an officer to make an arrest, the crime does not have to be committed in his presence. The officer has the right to arrest the abuser based on observations at the crime scene. The officer considers physical injuries, statements by the victim, children, and/or other witnesses, property damage, the overall condition of the residence at the time he arrived, and comes to a decision about whether or not to arrest the abuser. If you are holding an order of protection, the officer will also try to determine if there has been a violation of that order. If the officer feels there is enough evidence, he will then inform the offender (if he is present) that he is being arrested and state the charge(s). The officer will then handcuff the abuser and read him his rights. The officer will then take the abuser to the police station, where he is fingerprinted, photographed, and placed in a holding cell. Every police department has its own specific procedures and all law enforcement agencies usually comply with state laws. Again, how a department handles domestic violence cases will depend on where you live. The abuser may be eye-bonded out—i.e., required to post only his driver's license after he is processed and given a court date at the police station. From there he will be free to return to the residence pending a court hearing. The abuser may also be held overnight in jail while waiting to appear before a judge the following morning. Some states also have provisions called NO CONTACT or 72-HOUR-STAY-AWAY ORDERS. These orders can be issued by a judge, and they can be a condition for release from jail by the police.

NO-CONTACT OR 72-HOUR-STAY-AWAY ORDERS

A 72-hour-stay-away order is an order requiring the abuser to have no contact with you for 72 hours following his arrest. When issued this order, the abuser is asked to sign a document stating that he understands and acknowledges receipt and will comply with the order. Acceptance of this order can be a condition for his release.

A no-contact order can be issued for a longer period of time. It can also order the abuser to specifically stay away from the home, school, or other places the victim goes. In addition, this order can prohibit the abuser from sending letters, flowers, and gifts, or placing phone calls to your home, work, or friends you have contact with on a regular basis.

PRESSING CHARGES AGAINST
THE ABUSER

Over the past few years across the country, states have enacted policies called mandatory arrest.* That means that when a responding officer arrives at a crime scene, he has the ability to arrest the abuser without the victim filing charges. The officer has the power to press charges on behalf of the state. If the officer has reason, or what is referred to as "probable cause," to make an arrest, you must do your best to cooperate.

---

* *I do not believe that mandatory arrest should exist. It takes away the victim's right to choose. When a victim is in a violent relationship her rights have been taken away by her abuser. The legal system adds an additional burden when it dictates the nature of the abuse by taking away her right to choose whether or not she will press charges against her abuser.*

This can be good for you because in this situation the abuser believes that the "bad guy" is the system and not you. Many times an abuser will talk the victim into dropping the charges. He may tell you "I'm sorry, it won't happen again" or "I love you." (My favorite is "You can't do this, what about the kids, our family, you said we'd be together forever.") If charges are pressed by the state, you have no choice about whether or not he is charged and you must appear in court. Even if the two of you kiss and make up, the only people who can dismiss the charges are the attorney provided by the state and the judge. If the trial proceeds, you must remember that the abuser has committed a crime and that these laws were passed for your protection.

COUNSELING

If you haven't begun counseling, now is a good time to start. Being healthy and able to make good decisions is vital to your overall ability to get on with your life. Taking that first step is key. Let's say your abuser has just been arrested for domestic battery and the police are pressing the charges. Many women are happy that the abuser is in jail, while others feel guilty for having caused all this trouble or for what they have done. Please remember that you have done nothing that warrants the emotional or physical harm he has inflicted on you. That's why getting counseling is so important. In counseling you will learn what you are responsible for and what you are *not* responsible for.

Here's an example of someone who had her husband arrested and sought help:

Dear Project:Protect,

I am writing to say thank you. I recently saw you on a television program explaining the importance of getting out of abusive relationships and what a woman should do in order to live a healthy, normal life. After twenty-one years of both physical and verbal abuse, I was at the end of my rope. When we'd argue he would always blame me, saying things like "It's your own fault, you know, if you had listened to me in the first place we wouldn't be having this conversation." Or after he'd hit me he'd say "See, see what I had to do just so you would listen." I'm a grown woman forty-five years old, I work for a Fortune 500 company and I'm in upper management. I have no problem communicating with my coworkers or others. I realized he had the problem, not me. But I felt awkward seeking assistance. Then, when I was listening to you, I realized that it was my own pride standing in the way of reaching out for help. I did as you suggested. I got the phone book and in the yellow pages I found a women's helpline number. They directed me to counseling services in my area.

They even provided me with a list of lawyers for a divorce. Because my income was fairly substantial, I was lucky to receive good legal services. I realize that many women who you assist are not as fortunate. It's been eight months since I left my husband. My self-esteem has returned after twenty-one years of abuse. My soon-to-be ex-husband is now trying to win me back. He's sending gifts and flowers just as he did when we were dating. I'm still in love with him and my counselor says it will be a long time before I stop having guilty thoughts for leaving him.

Thank you for being there!

Counseling services for victims of abuse are available and often free. Taking that first step can make all the difference in your life and the lives of your children.

WHAT IF YOU ARE IN A RELATIONSHIP WITH A POLICE OFFICER?

In too many cases there is a clear reluctance on the part of the responding officers to use their techniques in the homes of fellow officers. The understanding that "blue defends blue" and the "code of silence" are very real concerns for women in relationships with police officers. The responding officer's hesitation to deal professionally with this type of crime can lead to disaster. All across America domestic violence in homes of police officers is one of the most underreported crimes.

In the August 1, 1992, *Chicago Defender,* Tony Kubicki, program coordinator of Milwaukee's Batterers Anonymous— Beyond Abuse, blamed improper screening for the recruitment of cops who are considered violent toward their families. Kubicki said, "Cops are members of their own elitist society. They are sworn to secrecy, promising not to penalize one of their own."

Is he above the law because he can carry a gun? Because there is no information on women in relationships—married or otherwise—with police officers, we have no idea of the frequency of abuse, but we do know that it happens and that these women are at a higher risk of being ignored by law enforcement than other women. Remember that the wife of a police officer is entitled to the same rights and treatment as any other person.

One officer's wife made a wry comment: "There are many benefits to being married to a police officer. You can receive discounts at stores on merchandise; the loan officer at a bank considers you a good credit risk; the department provides good medical benefits; and if your husband loses his life in the line of duty, you will be free to live your life once again as a human being, not a prisoner of war."

It is often difficult to deal with abuse victims who are married to anyone in law enforcement. Many police departments around the country have employee assistance programs and many victims don't even know they exist. Many police officers are reluctant to go. It looks bad. It's a pride thing, an ego thing. Policemen develop a macho, larger-than-life feeling when they carry that badge and gun. And some, not all, can't turn it off when they get home. Their wives/partners must be taught how to cope with the stress of being an officer's wife, how to defuse violence, and where to go if they need help. I believe the best way to help the families of police officers is to create a separate entity outside the department to handle the problem of violence in their homes. The internal affairs officers in police departments, except in particularly flagrant cases, usually find that nothing improper has occurred. However, at present we have to work to change that and absolutely insist that these programs be responsive to women who need them.

WHERE TO HIDE?

Law enforcement regularly receives information on the location of domestic violence abuse shelters. Consequently, if you are married to a police officer and seek refuge in a shelter, your husband may know exactly where to find you. Additionally, shelter workers are sometimes intimidated by someone with a badge and a gun knocking at the door. It is important to have an alternate plan, such as going to a hotel in another town or going to the home of a friend whom your husband doesn't know.

ARE POLICE OFFICERS DIFFERENT?

You have to understand that not all police officers are abusive. Being a police officer is one of the most demanding of all professions. The daily pressures placed upon the individual police officer creates stress. Across the country police officers constantly confront the worst examples of human behavior. A police officer is expected to be in control no matter what the situation. As one officer who was interviewed stated, "We act out this disposition—taking control—every time we respond to a call for help or observe a crime. Once we decide on a course of action, there is the badge, the gun, and the backup (from other officers) to enforce the law. And although our actions may be questioned later, in the heat of the moment we are in control."

Taking control is the very soul of what it means to be a police officer. It would take a rare, gifted person to keep the many difficulties that he or she encounters every day from spilling into his or her private life. Families of officers are also under constant pressure because of shift work, changing days off, court time, or sudden changes of plans due to unexpected work. All of this affects the entire family and/or the relationship. When police officers are trained at the academy, they learn how to respond to domestic violence calls. But when some officers respond to a domestic call in a police home, most wives we spoke with said either they were ignored, laughed at, or, in some cases, arrested to "teach them a lesson."

Police wives we interviewed across the country indicated that the actions (or nonactions) of the law enforcement community have not been a solution to their problems. The solution will come when police departments everywhere provide more counseling for their officers under stress and deal with violent officers as criminals.

SEEKING MEDICAL SERVICES

According to the Surgeon General in a report published by the U.S. Health Service in 1992, between 1.8 and 4 million American women are abused in their homes each year. The American Medical Association have set guidelines for diagnosing and treating domestic violence. They have developed protocols for identifying and assisting victims of abuse in emergency rooms, obstetrics and gynecology, pediatrics, and primary care settings. The National Coalition of Physicians Against Family Violence established by the American Medical Association now provides diagnostic and treatment guidelines for domestic violence patients.

When you seek medical attention for injuries inflicted by your abuser, keep in mind that the person who treats you is not there to judge you. His or her main objective is to provide you with sensitive care and treatment.

Many women go to hospital emergency rooms because it's a change to be in a safe environment for a while and away from the abuser. And many women don't believe that calling the police is a good alternative to their situation. Because many hospitals are now trained in domestic violence, they can offer a wide range of referrals to victims of abuse.

WHAT IF THE ABUSER INSISTS ON GOING TO THE HOSPITAL WITH YOU?

If the abuser takes you to the hospital, he may insist on being with you while you are being treated for your injuries. It's generally hospital policy, especially if the doctor or nurse suspects you may have been hurt by this person, to have him placed in the waiting area. If he refuses and says things like "That's my wife" or "That's my woman" or that he has a right to be with you, or if the hospital senses or suspects you are being treated for domestic violence, they will call hospital security. If the police take you to the hospital and they are pressed for time and want a statement or a report from you immediately, no matter what they tell you, they are not allowed to be present during your examination.

Going to the hospital is also a good way to document your injuries. Hospitals take pictures of your injuries and collect torn clothing for evidence in case you press charges against the abuser. The doctor who examines you will also make out a report, which you should get a copy of when you leave.

If you are afraid to return home, the police are required to transport you to a women's shelter, friend's, or relative's home. The police can also take you back home for clothes or medication you might need should you decide to stay somewhere else even if the abuser has not been arrested or has already bonded out.

making the decision to leave

ONE OF THE MAJOR REASONS women stay in abusive relationships is FEAR. They are afraid of what will happen to them and their children if they leave. Their fears are often justified; a woman is at greater risk of injury after she leaves an abusive relationship than if she stays.

If the victim has children, she may fear that she can't adequately provide for her children's financial, physical, and emotional needs if she leaves the relationship. She often decides to stay with the abuser for the "welfare of the children." She often fears the backlash of her extended family. She may have been raised and socialized to salvage a relationship at all costs and so see the dissolution of her relationship as a failure on her part. Motivated by pity and compassion, the victim may feel that she is the only person who can help the perpetrator overcome his abusive behaviors. If a victim was exposed to abuse or incest during her own childhood, she may accept these behaviors as "normal." Many women assume that other relationships are also abusive.

The emotional, verbal, and physical abuse a victim endures is similar to the torture experienced by prisoners of war. The victim often feels shame, humiliation, helplessness, and low self-esteem. She often identifies with her abuser and believes there is no way to escape. According to the U.S. Surgeon General, domestic violence may be the single most important context for female alcoholism, attempted suicide, rape and child abuse, homelessness for women and children, and a major contributor to a range of mental health problems.

The wide range of reasons women remain in abusive relationships include:

- She believes that she cannot make it on her own.
- She believes that staying is better than being on the streets without food or money.
- She believes that being divorced is a sign of failure.
- She believes that the law will do nothing to protect her.
- She believes that abuse is her partner's way of showing affection.
- She believes that he won't hurt her and will eventually change.
- She believes that her material possessions—car, house, money—compensate for his abuse.
- She believes those who know the abuser will not believe him capable of abuse.
- She believes that a woman's place is by her husband's side.

- She believes that without her he will fall apart.

- She believes that it's wrong to split up a family.

- She believes that God will make him better and keep her safe.

- She believes that she is worthless.

- She believes that in one form or another all relationships are abusive.

- She believes that to ask for outside assistance means she is at fault.

- She believes that she will lose her family and friends if she leaves.

- She believes her partner will make life miserable for her if she leaves.

- She believes that her children will be taken away.

- She believes that she will be turned away from the church.

- She believes that if she leaves, he will find her, and if he finds her, he will kill her.

WHAT ABOUT THE CHILDREN WHO GROW UP IN THESE HOMES?

"Someday maybe there will exist a well-informed, well-considered and yet fervent public conviction that

> *the most deadly of all possible sins is the mutilation of a child's spirit."*

> —Erik H. Erikson

Anybody who thinks that children are not affected by violence in the home is very mistaken. There is nothing, absolutely nothing, more terrifying than hearing your parents scream at each other in anger. And that terror is magnified tenfold when you see your father, whom you love, beating, knocking, bashing, and kicking the mother you adore.

As a child, you want to make it stop; after rushing to your mother's aid and getting knocked across the room yourself a few times, you learn to run away from the mayhem rather than toward it. Your feelings then become confused, swirling between the fear of being hurt yourself and the even worse dread that your mother will be killed if you don't make him stop. In your mind you start to feel responsible for the destruction. "If I can't make it stop, then it must be my fault."

The first time you experience it, the horror is unimaginable. Your whole warm, safe, comfortable world is exploding in front of your eyes. How can this be? Why is this happening?

PROFILE OF AN ABUSED CHILD

I didn't identify with victims of abuse until I began working with women who had been battered and their children who had witnessed the battering. I learned that the same "problems" I had suffered as a child in a violent home are still commonplace among these children thirty years later.

Thumbsucking was a treasured part of my life until I was about six years old. I quit only after my father repeatedly covered my thumb with castor oil. I wet my bed at least twice a week until I was nine years old. In elementary school I was unable to concentrate and many times fell asleep in class because we had been kept awake the night before by my father's violence. I was very disruptive in school, disturbing the other students while the teacher was instructing the class. I was always fighting, not only during school recess, but also in the streets and the local parks. I was known for giving the best black eye in the neighborhood.

I recall being angry all the time and learned to express my anger away from home, where I could get away with my behavior. I also chewed my nails until they bled. When my mother would tell me to stop biting my nails, the only way I could leave them alone was by sitting on my hands. I remember that she offered me whatever I wanted if I would quit. I was nineteen years old before I stopped biting my nails.

I thought my behavior and the actions of my family were normal. It wasn't until I began spending time at the homes of my friends' families that I realized that either they were crazy or we were.

Like most children, I felt guilty about the violence. I believed that I was either the direct cause or at least a major part of the reason things weren't going right in our house. I took personal responsibility for the abuse, telling myself:

· If only I had cleaned my room like I was supposed to, they wouldn't be arguing.

· If only I had protected my mom, this wouldn't have happened.

· If only I had called 911, it could have been stopped.

· If only I hadn't been born, things would be better.

· If only I was a better student in school . . .

· If only I didn't talk back so much . . .

· If only I could tell somebody . . .

· If only, if only, if only . . .

PARENTS' RESPONSIBILITIES

Parents must consider what kind of example they are setting for their children. Adults often decide that by keeping the family together, they are doing what is best for the children. However, children who are reared in violent homes learn to use violence as their method of problem solving and coping. To grow up, as I did, in a family where your father repeatedly beats your mother, is indeed a devastating experience with a lifetime of damaging consequences.

The psychological scars children develop from watching their fathers beat their mothers are just as damaging as those formed from being physically abused themselves. We carry into our adult relationships what we have learned of family life as children because our earliest and most significant role models were our parents. The secrecy we learned in abusive homes is replayed in other areas such as work and friendships.

We adult children of violent homes are accommodating and cooperative because we always fear retaliation. We've learned not to acknowledge tension or stress and expend a lot of effort trying to avoid problems, often telling lies to prevent ourselves or others from getting hurt. We can be disorganized and directionless. What we are doing to children who grow up in these homes is confusing and misleading them. The result is that we are passing the baton for them to either be abused or abusive when they grow up.

I interviewed children who were in shelters with their mothers. I was curious as to why they thought their father was abusive in the home. I posed five fairly simple questions, and here's how over sixty children answered me:

1. *Question:* What does your mommy do that makes your daddy get so angry?

   Answers:

   · Mommy made Daddy angry.

   · Mommy doesn't listen when Daddy tells her to do something.

   · Mommy doesn't come back from the store like Daddy asked.

   · Mommy was a bad girl.

   · Mommy didn't clean the house.

2. *Question:* Do you think Daddy is angry because he works too much?

    Answers:

    · He's under a lot of pressure, because when he comes home he's mad.

    · Sometimes, but it's because dinner wasn't ready when he came home.

    · Daddy and Mommy were fighting because I got in trouble at school.

    · Because my daddy's always working.

    · Because my daddy comes home drunk.

3. *Question:* Do you and your mom keep secrets?

    Answers:

    · Mommy says I'm old enough to keep a secret.

    · Mommy says I can't tell anybody my daddy is mean to us.

    · Mommy says I can't tell anybody. If I do, everybody will think I lie and liars don't go to heaven.

    · Mommy says what Daddy does is our little secret.

4. *Question:* What do you think would happen to you if you told someone that Daddy has been hurting you or Mommy?

Answer:

- Mommy says that people will take me away someplace else to live.
- I'm not allowed to tell anybody or I'll get punished.
- Very bad things will happen to me and my mommy.
- I won't get to see them ever again.

5. *Question:* Why do you think Daddy gets so mad at Mommy?

Answer:

- Because my daddy loves us.
- 'Cause nobody ever listens to him.
- I don't know. I get punished when I'm bad, so does Mommy.
- Because Mommy is always tired.

If you are a victim of abuse and you have children, look at the answers to the questions that we asked. Read each one carefully. If you weren't sure about doing something before, please consider it now.

Deciding to leave doesn't mean your world is at an end,

it's probably just beginning. Many times women say to themselves "I'll wait until the children get older." Someplace within yourself find the strength to get out. Recognizing that *he* is the cause of the abuse and *not you* will be the first step.

WHERE DO I BEGIN?

You can start by doing something for yourself each day, simple things like drawing a bath after everyone is asleep, sitting and soaking doing absolutely nothing, thinking only good thoughts. You could make an appointment to have your hair or nails done. Plan a walk every day to a place that is relaxing for you. Schedule coffee or have a meal with a family member or friend. Incorporate one or two things just for yourself into your daily routine. Whether it's twenty minutes or two hours, make an appointment with yourself for just you. If you are under stress and pressure at home or work, you will not be as effective as you could be. Think about how you feel after a good night's sleep. When you get up in the morning you are ready for anything, because you've recharged yourself.

When we assist women, the first thing they have to do is set aside time to do something wonderful for themselves. Most women are skeptical at first saying things like "I didn't call you for help so you could tell me to take a bath." Some have grown angry and hung up the phone. Or they've said, "That's not going to help me" or "You've got to be joking." So our next question to them: "WHEN IS THE LAST TIME YOU DID

SOMETHING SPECIAL FOR YOURSELF?" Ah, total silence on the other end of the phone. Some women said it had been years, others replied that the thought never even crossed their mind. After just a few weeks, most women realized that this mini exercise had made a difference.

YOU ARE NOT ALONE

Even people who are wealthy and famous can be victims of domestic violence. Tina Turner, the popular singer, is an example. Despite her apparent success as a well-known entertainer, wife, and mother, she was smothered by the tight control of Ike Turner, her husband. He beat her on a regular basis for not doing what he wanted and took control of her finances. She was abused by a man who professed to love her. After many years, Tina finally found the strength and courage to leave. Despite her wealth and fame as a successful entertainer, she was so determined to get away that she left with nothing more than a belief in herself and the clothes on her back. After leaving a situation in which she was regularly disrespected and beaten, Tina achieved even greater popularity and wealth than she ever had with Ike.

If you believe in yourself, you can start over no matter what your current circumstances are. We must promise ourselves that:

- We as women will no longer be the "silent minority." We will be the vocal majority.
- We have two goals: To take care of ourselves, and Be SAFE.
- We will not be controlled, harassed, verbally abused, raped, or murdered at the hands of those who profess to love us.
- Together, we will be victorious in our journey.

12 STEPS TO RENEWAL

FOR THE SAKE OF OURSELVES, WE

1. Believe that there is a power greater than our own selves and that we can leave an abusive relationship.

2. Believe and understand that FEAR is a four-letter word that someone else inflicts on us.

3. Believe that we can gain the strength and knowledge to overcome the fear instilled in us by those who want to manipulate and harm us.

4. Believe that there are those who try to take away our goals and dreams because they feel they have a right to them.

5. Believe that anyone who must use violence to make a point is a coward.

6. Believe that we are special, unique gifts born to this world.

7. Believe that we all have a right to live without the constant threat of violence.

8. Believe that we can get out of a violent, unhealthy relationship and that no one else can control our destinies.

9. Believe that violent acts inflicted upon us are not our responsibility, but belong to the perpetrator.

10. Believe that by taking control for our own lives we can break the cycle of violence not only for ourselves, but for our children as well.

11. Believe that we are not responsible for being hurt. We can control only ourselves.

12. Believe that we are not alone. TOGETHER, WE CAN FACE ANYTHING!

The book *A Return to Love* by Marianne Williamson defines everything we are. This book teaches us how to love ourselves. It can assist you in learning how to cope with your everyday life. At our agency, *A Return to Love* has been part of the healing process for women we have assisted.

the escape plan

ONCE YOU HAVE MADE the decision to leave, the first thing you need to do is to create an escape plan. When you start forming your escape plan, you begin to regain control from your abuser. The key factor here is to make choices and set long-range goals. Your abuser believes that he has total control over everything in your life. Once he learns that he no longer has control over you, i.e., that the relationship is over, you could be in great danger. So before you go anywhere, you need a plan of action.

In preparation for your escape, gather the following items and put them in a safe place outside your home. (Consider giving them to a friend or relative whom you trust.)

- Birth certificates for you and your children
- Insurance policies
- Marriage certificate

- Medical records
- Children's vaccination records
- Dental records for you and your children
- Passports for you and your children
- Prescriptions for any medications you and your children take. (If possible, try to stock up.)
- Eyeglasses or hearing aid devices/information
- School records for the children
- Social security cards (or numbers) for you and the children
- Spare keys to the house, garage, car, etc.
- Title to the car
- Copy of your most recent credit report (call your local credit bureau)
- Copy of any personal phone books
- Anything you may have on computer disks (be sure to check the hard drive)

It is also important that you save as much money as you can.

Don't be in a rush to gather everything all at once. Do it safely, one step at a time. Incorporate this time into your plan of action.

You will also need to gather information on your abuser. You may wonder why you need this information. There are many reasons. Let's say that after you have left, he tries to harm you in some way. Maybe you will need to make out a police report or obtain a court order of protection. The more information you provide a police officer or an officer of the court, the easier it will be to either have him arrested or served with an order of protection. You will also need certain information if you are planning to file for divorce. Many women have little to no knowledge of their financial situation. They know only that there has always been enough money in their checking account to pay bills. Some don't even know what their partner's income is. In most cases when you get divorced, you are entitled to half of what he has. With all of the pertinent information, an attorney can investigate further and ensure you receive a fair settlement in your divorce agreement.

You also need to take information about your credit card balances with you. It is not uncommon, especially when you file for divorce, to discover that the balances owed on your joint credit cards have reached their limits. It most probably means that your abuser has gone on a spending frenzy. However, you bear half of the responsibility for the debt incurred even though you had no knowledge of it and had left the residence. Unless you have your name removed from the card(s) as a signer or obtain your own credit cards, the burden of debt will fall upon you when the settlement agreement is prepared. Half that money owed will come out of your pocket. With divorces also come child support payments. There are many parents who try to avoid paying child support at all costs. In order for the courts to effectively enforce a court-ordered monthly support payment, they need the parents' social security numbers and other personal information. This allows the court system to ensure payments are made to you by holding his wages or IRS refunds.

INFORMATION ABOUT YOUR ABUSER
YOU NEED TO TAKE WITH YOU

- Social security number
- Driver's license number
- Credit card information—i.e., account numbers and current balances
- Pay stubs
- Work information, including address and phone number
- Addresses of family members and friends
- Criminal history (if any) and all documents pertaining to that history
- Bank accounts (if he has a personal checking account, tear out a deposit slip from the checkbook, it has the account number on it)
- Vehicle he drives with make, model, color, plate number
- A recent photo—try to have more than just one picture

If you have been injured by the abuser during the course of your relationship, make sure to gather all copies of medical and/or police reports and court orders of protection. This information can play an important role in your divorce case, custody case, or when filing charges against the abuser. In many instances you will be asked for any prior history of abuse.

FINANCIAL AND OTHER RECORDS YOU SHOULD TAKE WITH YOU

- All bank account numbers, including any accounts in your children(s) name. Try to get copies of a few recent statements.
- Credit union account information
- 401K plan information
- Profit-sharing information
- Safe deposit box information (Do you have a spare key?)
- Any and all copies of title(s) to car
- Copies of your income tax returns for the last three years
- Copies of any deed(s) to property held either jointly or separately
- Copies of any outstanding loan documents. Write down the amounts of your monthly payments.

- All credit cards, both those held jointly and those held separately (make a record of the balances)
- A couple of his paycheck stubs
- Copies of your/his signature card(s) on file at the bank (go to the bank and request this information)
- Copies of any stock certificates held in all your names, including those belonging to your children
- Copies of savings bonds and/or certificate(s) of deposit
- Copies of your court order of protection (make extra copies)
- All insurance policies, including your children's
- Copies of your will(s)
- Copies of any trust fund information
- Pension information
- Copies of canceled checks (listed month by month) for the past five years

Make THREE copies of all these documents (and anything else that you feel is important). Keep one set yourself, keep one with a trusted friend or in a safe deposit box, and give a third set to your attorney.

The day you are leaving, unless you are told otherwise by an attorney, take half of any and all related assets that have been acquired during your marriage. These assets include bonds, checking or savings accounts, and charge cards. Once you leave you can be certain the first thing your abuser will do is withdraw or freeze any accounts that include your name on them. It is also important that you consult with a certified tax accountant. Whatever settlement money you receive, such as property, luxury items, assets, etc., there are tax ramifications. You need to know how this will affect you and you need to incorporate this into your plan of action.

MAKING A LIST

You are now ready to sit down and make your lists. First make a list of all personal items you are planning to take with you. Then list the items you plan to take for your children. Remember to include any toys or blankets they are especially fond of. Also, make a list of any items that have sentimental value.

Slowly begin to take these items out of the residence. Don't take everything at once, do it slowly. If you're planning to take family photos or artwork from the home, be ready with an answer when he asks after these items. For pictures, say you lent them to a friend or relative. For the artwork, say you sent it out to be reframed. You know this person better than anyone else. If he is quick to notice when items are missing, don't take the chance until you are ready to go. And remember, no item is worth more than your life.

If you can afford to rent a storage facility for items that you know won't be missed, then go ahead. Otherwise ask someone you trust if you can store your things in his or her basement. Be careful when you pack and don't mark the boxes. The fewer people who know what's going on, the better.

You should also make a list of all your monthly living expenses. Create a realistic budget for yourself, listing the following items:

- Food
- Rent/mortgage
- Taxes
- All utilities
- Insurance for car, home, health, and life
- Medical services for doctor, dentist, and prescriptions
- Transportation costs for bus, train, gas, parking, tolls, repairs
- Child care
- Clothing
- School costs for tuition, books, supplies, etc.

LEAVING WITH CHILDREN

If you are leaving a relationship in which children are involved, it is important that you consult with an attorney to learn the laws in your state regarding child endangerment and kidnapping, so that you can avoid being accused of these things. If you cannot afford to speak with a private attorney, you can call the American Bar Association (its number is listed in the yellow pages). You can also call any legal aid service or legal aid bureau. Inform the attorney you speak with that you are a battered woman. The attorney may provide you with names of experts who assist women fleeing the state with their children. Or he/she can offer support group and counseling information. Each state's laws are different, so you will have to investigate on your own. It's generally a good idea to prepare a few questions ahead of time before speaking with an attorney. You should also keep a written log with names and telephone numbers of everyone that you called.

If you believe that your life and the lives of your children are in danger, you need to take legal measures to remove your children from the situation, otherwise you could face legal repercussions. I'll give you an example. You are married with two small children. Your partner's violence is escalating. The police have been called on a regular basis by someone in the house or a neighbor. Although you are not causing the abuse, you are guilty of endangering your own children. It doesn't matter that they haven't been physically harmed, they have witnessed firsthand verbal and/or physical abuse. If a responding officer feels the children could be in danger, he can call the child welfare agency in your state and the children can be removed and handed over to the state's care pending a hearing in juvenile court. If enough calls are placed regarding the safety of your children, the state has an obligation to investigate their welfare. It does not matter that you are not abusive. The fact that violence is occurring in your household is sometimes enough reason to remove your children. You have to be the one who removes them from this dangerous environment before someone else does.

On the other hand, unless you follow proper legal channels, you can be charged with kidnapping if you take your child out of the state. All states have child abduction laws on the books, and many offenders will try to use these laws to their own advantage. Let's say you are involved in an abusive relationship and you decide to take the kids out of the state for an extended period of time. The offender is angry that you are not there. He wants you to return home with the kids. He tells you not to try his patience, and demands that you return immediately. In certain circumstances he is within his rights to call the police (even though he knows where you are) and say you've abducted the children and your whereabouts are unknown. He starts the ball rolling by calling the police and filing a missing person's report. Then the authorities are notified and you could be charged with kidnapping and child abduction, both federal offenses. I'm not trying to scare you, but it does happen. Although this may seem supremely unfair, a legal catch-22 in which you are damned if you do and damned if you don't, protect yourself from future hardship by being aware of the laws that govern your mobility with your children.

No matter what an offender has done or how abusive he has been to you, the courts usually do not deny him visitation privileges or strip him of his parental rights. If you are legally married and you flee to a battered women's shelter with your children, or if you are taken to a shelter by the police, that will be all right. By doing so the abuse is documented. Again, check with the legal services available so you know and understand all your options.

THE ROLE OF AN ATTORNEY

When you decide to end your relationship, you may need to contact an attorney. If you are filing for a divorce or your partner has filed for one, you need representation and should seek legal assistance. The attorney who represents you will do so in civil court (See definitions, pages 126–36). It is important that you understand the role of an attorney.

When a domestic violence victim is married and decides to leave the relationship and dissolve the marriage, she needs to retain a civil attorney. The job of a civil attorney is to handle your divorce and the distribution of marital property. In situations where children are involved, the attorney will also handle your custody case.

If you need an attorney but can't afford to pay for one, you can call the American Bar Association listed in the yellow pages or the nearest legal assistance agency. Every state has a legal assistance agency, and if you have little or no income, you may qualify for their services. The agency may be able to handle your case on a pro bono basis (no charge) or refer you to someone who will take your case.

If you can afford to hire your own attorney, you should select someone with whom you feel comfortable. Your friends, family, coworkers, or the local bar association can make suggestions, but the final decision is yours. Try to identify an attorney who has prior experience with domestic violence and make an appointment for an initial consultation (this may be free). It's also a good idea to take along a trusted friend. This person can take notes for you and give you feedback on the meeting.

Prepare for the initial consultation by writing down a list of questions. Don't be afraid to ask a lot of questions and be prepared to take some notes during the consultation. Do not try to remember everything the attorney says, just write it down. And whatever you do, speak up, and don't be embarrassed. You are there to interview the attorney, not the other way around. The attorney is not there to sit in judgment of you or criticize what you say or do. If that should happen, politely say thank you and walk out. Don't bring any of the documents about your financial status until you've decided who you want to hire.

The following is a list of questions you may want to ask the attorney:

- What percentage of your practice is devoted to divorce?
- How long have you been an attorney?
- Do you know the laws pertaining to domestic violence and stalking?
- Are you experienced in filing court orders of protection?
- What is your experience in handling child custody cases?

- Have you ever dealt with women who have been abused?

- What is your hourly rate?

- What is your billing rate for telephone calls to clients or others in a divorce case?

- Will you be handling my case entirely, or will others be working on my case?

- Will an itemized bill be sent on a monthly basis?

- Will you inform me when complications arise or of strategies you will take as the case proceeds?

- Will I be expected to pay the full rate when nonattorneys are answering questions or when others are assisting me?

- How much money will be required initially?

- How familiar are you with tax laws pertaining to divorce settlements?

MOVING OUT

When the time arrives to actually move out, try to do it with the assistance of as many people as possible. Schedule your move for a time when you know the offender will not be around. Do not ask for help from a friend or relative whose loyalty to the abuser may lead him/her to tell the abuser that you are leaving. Rent or borrow a truck or van to transport your things and arrange for storage of your items, if possible. If you have a court order of protection, call your local law enforcement agency and ask that they send an officer to be present while you are moving.

If you move within the same state and fear your abuser may try to track you down, the following are some steps that can make it difficult for him to find you:

Utilities. Make all calls regarding service changes from a pay phone or a friend's phone in case your calls are being monitored. Select an address other than the one where you reside and have all mail rerouted. If you are employed, have utility bills sent to your work address and ask that your home address not be indicated in their system. If you don't have a job, have these bills sent to you in care of a friend or relative. Or rent a private mailbox and use the word "suite" in front of your box number. I don't recommend U.S. postal boxes because they can be traced easily.

When establishing new utility services, call the company and ask to speak to a supervisor. Explain that your life is in danger and that you are requesting that a security code known only to you be assigned to your account. Ask that no one be allowed to change account information or be given information about your account without the use of the security code. Wait a few days and call the utility company back and ask for information without using the code just to make sure the request has been entered into your account information.

Monthly checks or dividends: If you receive monthly payments such as workmen's compensation, call and ask to speak to a supervisor. Explain to the supervisor that you are in danger and ask that your documentation be kept confidential. Write down the name of the person you spoke with and send him or her a certified letter confirming your request.

Other traceable records: You can also be located through your voter registration since this information is part of the public record—i.e., this information is available to those who submit a written request. You income tax return can also be a traceable record. At tax time, file your return under a different address. The Internal Revenue Service does not require that you use your residential address. Medical prescriptions for drugs, hearing devices, or eyeglasses can also be traceable. Avoid using your home address and phone number on these forms. Use work or other "safe" address(es) instead.

Remember, increased computerization of government offices makes the process of searching for someone much easier.

FINDING SOMEWHERE TO LIVE

Planning to relocate is not easy. It can be time-consuming, costly, and, most of all, stressful. When renting an apartment, most owners require that you fill out an application and some even require a small fee to do a credit history check. If you are trying not to be found, there are some tips you should follow:

· Ask someone you know and trust to apply for the apartment on your behalf.

- Check to see if you know anyone in apartment management or rental who could assist you.
- Obtain copies of neighborhood newspapers outside of your area for listings.
- Look on bulletin boards at grocery stores outside of your area.
- Find someone that the abuser doesn't know whom you can temporarily move in with.
- Drive around neighborhoods with a pen and paper in hand and write down "for rent" address and telephone numbers.
- Get up as early as possible, get the newspaper, and start calling ads in the apartment real estate section.

RELOCATION WITH FEW OR NO RESOURCES

This can be achieved; it just takes patience and work. Begin by calling your local battered women shelters for housing available in your area. I have also found that churches are good resources for housing. Get the yellow pages out and start calling.

You can also call your city or county Department of Human Resources (they are also listed in the yellow pages). They provide all sorts of services and referrals such as:

- Housing
- Job training
- Employment classes
- Employment services for displaced homemakers
- On-the-job training

Contact the State Department of Employment Security where you live. It can direct you to other programs in the area.

WHEN PLACING TELEPHONE CALLS

It is very important when you are making arrangements to leave that you place your calls from someplace other than where you are living. Once you have relocated and you call friends or relatives, do it from a place away from where you have relocated. Because of modern technology, it's very easy for someone to call you back by entering a code in the phone. You don't want to risk having your abuser find out your home phone number.

SHELTERS

There are shelters available for battered women and/or their children. This is another temporary housing alternative.

Many programs provide more than just shelter. They can direct you to a new, safe way of life. Shelters provide beds, food, clothing, counseling, and the support of others who have fled their abusive situations. Some even provide second-stage housing, which are apartments or shared living spaces. A shelter provides you with a safe, clean, healthy environment. It could be your ticket out. To find a shelter to go to, begin by calling shelters in your area. They, upon request, will give you the telephone numbers of shelters outside your immediate area. The length of time you are allowed to stay in a shelter depends on where you call. At most shelters you can stay anywhere from two days to indefinitely, but each program has its own rules, so ask how long you can stay when you call. Be prepared to make a lot of phone calls. Many shelters will be full when you call. Each facility will most likely do an intake over the phone. Don't get upset by this process, it's pretty much standard procedure. The information you provide is confidential and everything you tell the person on the other end of the phone stays right there on the phone. Shelters can also advise you on how to obtain an order of protection, and how to apply for public assistance and food stamps. They are a tremendous resource for all victims of abuse. And the services they provide are free of charge.

TO HELP PLAN YOUR ESCAPE

Below I've included telephone numbers that will assist you in making your plans. Remember to place these calls from locations other than your residence. Try not to use credit cards or other personal information that might be tracked to you. It's also important to use an assumed name that you will be sure to remember after you leave.

TOLL-FREE NUMBERS

Auto Rentals

	National Numbers	Hearing Impaired (TDD)
Alamo Rent-A-Car	1-800-327-9633	1-800-522-9292
Avis Rent-A-Car	1-800-331-1212	1-800-331-2323
Budget Rent-A-Car	1-800-527-0700	1-800-826-5510
Dollar Rent-A-Car	1-800-421-6868	1-800-232-3301
National Car Rental	1-800-227-7368	1-800-328-6323
Thrifty Rent-A-Car	1-800-367-2277	1-800-358-5856

Bus Schedule Information and Reservations

America Tour & Travel	1-800-964-1640	
Greyhound	1-800-231-2222	1-800-345-3109
En Español Llame	1-800-531-5332	
Mid America	1-800-323-0312	

Trains

Amtrak	1-800-872-7245	1-800-523-6590

LOW-FARE LAST-MINUTE AIRLINE RESERVATIONS
FOR ALL AIRLINES

A Ticket 2 Fly	1-800-423-2359
1-800-FLY-4-Less	1-800-359-4537
1-800-FLY-Cheap	1-800-359-2432
1-800-FLY-ASAP	1-800-359-2727

AIRLINES

American	1-800-433-7300	1-800-543-1586
International	1-800-624-6262	
En Español Llame	1-800-633-3711	
Canadian Airlines		
International	1-800-426-7000	
Cayman Airways	1-800-422-9626	
Continental	1-800-525-0280	1-800-343-9195
International	1-800-231-0856	
Delta	1-800-241-4141	1-800-831-4488
International	1-800-221-1212	
Iberia Airlines of Spain	1-800-772-4642	
Kiwi Airlines	1-800-538-5494	
KLM Royal Dutch	1-800-374-7747	
Lufthansa	1-800-645-3880	
Northwest	1-800-225-2525	1-800-328-2298
International	1-800-447-4747	
Swiss Air	1-800-221-4750	

| United | 1-800-241-6522 | 1-800-323-0170 |
| U.S. Air | 1-800-428-4322 | 1-800-245-2966 |

NATIONWIDE MOVING COMPANIES

Active Van Lines	1-800-882-6436
Alliance	1-800-737-8968
Big O Moving &	
Storage	1-800-339-5951
Mini Moves	1-800-300-6683
New World Van Lines	1-800-422-9300

MOVING EQUIPMENT RENTAL

| Ryder | 1-800-GO-RYDER |
| U-Haul | 1-800-468-4285 |

STORAGE

| Public Storage | 1-800-447-8673 |

HOTELS AND RESERVATIONS

Days Inn	1-800-325-2525	1-800-343-9195
Embassy Suites	1-800-362-2779	1-800-458-4708
Excel	1-800-356-8013	
Fairfield Inn	1-800-228-2800	

Hampton Inn	1-800-426-7866	
Hilton	1-800-445-8667	
Holiday Inn	1-800-465-4329	1-800-368-1133
Howard Johnson	1-800-654-2000	1-800-654-8442
Hyatt	1-800-228-9000	1-800-228-9548
La Quinta Inn	1-800-531-5900	
Marriott	1-800-228-9290	1-800-228-7014
Omni	1-800-843-6664	1-800-541-0808
Pan Pacific	1-800-327-8585	
Radisson	1-800-333-3333	
Ramada	1-800-228-2828	1-800-345-2926
Red Roof Inn	1-800-843-7663	
Sheraton	1-800-325-3535	1-800-325-1717
Stouffer	1-800-468-3571	1-800-833-4747

CREDIT CARDS

American Express	1-800-528-4800
Diners Club	1-800-525-9150
Discover	1-800-347-2683
Visa	1-800-227-6800
MasterCard	1-800-632-4730

If you are hearing impaired, you can call the national relay service when you are trying to call a hearing person or business at 1-800-526-0844. This number is for hearing impaired only.

■

staying safe

EVEN AFTER YOU HAVE MOVED OUT, you must continue to be very careful. There are a number of precautions you can take to protect your security. First, don't tell anybody where you live or work, especially anybody who has a connection to your abuser. Don't fill out any questionnaires or surveys, no matter how innocent they seem. When planning a vacation or get-together with friends and family, keep your agenda private. If you are staying at a shelter or some kind of temporary housing, keep your location confidential.

Ask people in your new environment to keep information pertaining to your children's school, playmates, and caretakers confidential. You will be surprised at how supportive people can be. Instruct your family, friends, neighbors, and coworkers not to provide any information to anyone who might ask about you.

One of the most common ways abusers will use to find you is to go to one of your friends and say: "Someone in the family has just died. I must reach her immediately, would you have the number?" Your friend should reply no, even if he/she knows where you are. Then the abuser, who is very manipulative, may say, "I just want the telephone number, what harm is there in that? I am not asking for her address." The next thing you know, he's talked your friend into giving him your number and he's calling you. With the first three digits of your telephone number, a person can locate you or at least discover the general area in which you live.

The abuser may also ask one of your friends to give you something from him such as money, mail, or a message. This is not a good idea. Think about it for a moment. Your friend is being asked to bring something DIRECTLY to your door. Your abuser can follow this person and the next thing you know he's pounding on your door. Remind whoever you let into your confidence that although a random question may appear entirely innocent, they need to act as though they know nothing about how or where you can be reached, otherwise they could be jeopardizing your safety. You and they must be vigilant in protecting your privacy. I've seen too many situations where the above situations have happened.

Beware of calls about an emergency. Let's say someone close to you receives a call about one of your children. Perhaps this person is listed at the school as next of kin or someone to contact in case of an emergency. No matter who we are, we're all human and our first reflex is to react to any life-threatening situation. But if this person receives a call about an emergency, he or she must verify the information before heading out the door. Ask him or her to document the circumstances of the situation and get the caller's name and telephone number. Even if the caller claims he is the police, get a number. This can also happen in your workplace. Warn the people you work with to beware of these phone calls and tell them what they should do if they receive one.

You must also be leery of calls requesting your location in order to deliver flowers, gifts, express mail packages, or telegrams. These so-called deliveries and messengers are often the abuser trying to make contact with you. The abuser can even come as the messenger in disguise. If no one in your workplace knows what he looks like, he can walk right up to you and no one would know the difference. No matter how embarrassed you may feel, it is important to let others know what is going on. You'd be very surprised how supportive people can be.

Try to avoid a rock-solid routine. Any set routine makes it easier for him to know where you will be at any given time on any given day. This means alternating where you shop, exercise, take the kids to the park. Change your entire schedule whenever possible. If you are truly afraid he is trying to find you, don't leave your home or office without someone with you. Don't exit from the same door or at the exact same time when leaving either your home or office. Ask your employer if you can change or rotate your hours, making it harder to know where you'll be when. If you think you've been discovered, find out if the company you work for has other locations. Ask if you can be transferred and explain the reason. You shouldn't feel embarrassed or ashamed. The abuser is the one who has the problem, not you. You must think of your safety, not what others may think of you.

Try not to leave work alone, and ask security personnel or coworkers to walk with you to your vehicle. The security agent employed by your company isn't there to watch just for fire or theft. He is also there to ensure your safety while at work. It's very important to let the security personnel know your situation. Provide them with a recent photo of the abuser and the make and model of the car he may be driving. Ask them to walk you to your car and report any unusual activity to their supervisor. Perhaps the same car has been circling the area for a while. Maybe someone has even stopped by to ask questions about you. It could be as innocent as a parked van across the street that is out of place. A security person can help watch for any of this.

You also must have a plan in place. Let's say you are walking to your car and you see your abuser in the distance, heading in your direction. What will you do? The first step is not to panic. If you're with someone, point him out to that person and then turn around and walk back into the building and have someone contact the police. Have a code word ready when you are with others that will tell them your abuser is nearby. If someone sees you running, they should not go after the abuser, they need to call the police. Warn your office mates that if you are ostensibly in the bathroom for too long, there might be a problem and they should try to find out where you've gone. It's a good idea to know where all the emergency exits are located in the building and in all buildings you enter.

You should also teach your children what to do in an emergency. Give them a code word that they can easily remember. Practice a routine, make a game out of it. For example, tell them if the front window shade is down, they should not enter the house but go to a neighbor's home and ask to use the telephone and call the police. Teach them what to tell a neighbor or the police if you are in danger. Explain to your children that although you are in a situation that might be scary, regardless of what they hear, they should not feel bad leaving you. The most important thing they can do is not enter the house but go to get help.

If you can afford it, buy a portable phone and keep the number secret. This could be a life saver if your telephone lines are cut, or if you are being followed in your car. Remember to keep the phone charged and ready for use at all times.

CAR SAFETY

If possible, trade in your current vehicle for one he isn't familiar with and keep a spare set of keys handy. Magnetic key trays for hiding keys on the body of your car may be purchased at any auto parts store. Hide an extra key under the hood of your car by the windshield on the driver's side and put another beneath the driver's side wheel. Always examine your car before you enter it. Check to see if it has been tampered with by looking underneath the car for fluid leakage and/or nails. Car alarms are very affordable, you should buy one if you can.

Use the defensive driving technique SIPDE: SCAN, IDEN-TIFY, PREDICT, DECIDE, EXECUTE. Scan the area to see if you are being followed. Identify the car that is following you.

Try to predict what he will do, then decide how to respond. Execute your decision. If you are being followed while driving on the highway, drive in the center lane to make it more difficult for someone to drive you off the road.

When you are in danger, keep your hand on the horn and flash your lights. Drive to the nearest facility—police station, fire station, bank, or hospital—where there are armed guards on duty.

Don't hesitate to tell as many people as possible about what is going on in your life. Remember, you've done nothing wrong, so don't worry about what they are thinking. You and your children have a right to be safe, and keeping quiet about the violent circumstances does not help you; it only helps the abuser.

IF YOU STAY AND HE LEAVES

If you stay and he leaves, change all the locks to your residence and, if you can afford it, buy an alarm system for your home. If that isn't possible, consider some of the protective devices that can be purchased at your local hardware store.

Rearrange the furniture in your house so things are in unfamiliar places in the event he decides to break in. There are also simple but very effective ways to ensure that no one can enter your house without making a lot of noise. For example, you can take the bells from Christmas tree ornaments and string them on the back of every entryway to your home. You can use tin cans or your children's heavy toys and string them up over the curtain rods and windowsills, then anchor them to a heavy object in the room. You can also purchase special window locks from the hardware store. (Ask someone in the store for advice about which ones are the most effective.) Other entryways to your home can be blocked with large objects that make noise when moved. You can also set mousetraps, although you must be careful if you have small children to keep your children away from the traps.

When you are securing your home, don't forget basement windows and doors. Once you have started thinking in terms of your safety, you will no doubt come up with a variety of creative ways that will keep you and your children safe.

Keep yourself and your children away from the windows at all times. Change where they play in the house and where they watch their favorite television shows. If your abuser knows the household routine, he may try to break the window or make contact with the children by tapping on the window or knocking at the door when he knows they are around. If he does this, you should immediately go to a safe room in your home with the children and the portable phone and then contact the police.

Do not allow the children to play outside without supervision. Remember, he will do almost anything to get you to return to him. Many times he will use the children, even taking them, just to get your attention. The abuser has a plan and so must you.

IF HE BREAKS IN

If he should break in, dial 911 or the police, take the telephone, and throw it in a wastebasket and scream for your life. They'll come very quickly. Or leave the phone off the hook so someone can hear what is going on. Police respond immediately when it is absolutely clear that you are in a life-threatening situation.

If you call the police, try and get the name of the dispatcher that you've spoken with. Write down everything he or she tells you, including the case number and the name of the officer or station assigned. When the police arrive, and the offender is there, ask that YOUR rights be explained to the abuser. If the officer is not responsive, or refuses to make a report, call the station immediately and ask to speak with a supervisor or the watch commander on duty. Calmly explain that you believe that your case is not being handled properly, and that you wish to have another officer come out and take a report.

ADDITIONAL SUGGESTIONS FOR KEEPING
YOUR HOME SAFE

First go outside your home or the building where you live. Write down where all the entryways to your residence are—i.e., your front door, side door, basement or back door, garage door, and the number of windows.

If you live in a high-rise or large apartment building, check to see if there is a separate service or delivery entrance. If so, does the entrance allow access into the building? To your unit? Are all the doors locked twenty-four hours a day? Are they secure? Are the entryways to your home, apartment hallways, garage basement well lit?

Do you frequently keep tools or ladders outside? If tools or ladders are not kept locked up, they can be used to gain entry into your home. What about your neighbors or the building service people? Have they been alerted to contact you if they see someone trying to gain entry to your home.

What about bushes and trees? Do they cover up your house? Can someone easily hide in them? Look carefully when you are taking note of what should be done to the outside of your home.

Second, go inside your home and do the same thing. Check the windows to see if they are secure and if the locks are in good working condition. If you have no locks on your windows, it's probably wise to have some installed. Thumb-turn center locks, the ones that flip open by moving the lock from one side to another, can be opened easily. Hardware stores sell special locks for windows; go and investigate what is available. If you can afford them, buy separate locks for each window. It's a good idea to keep blinds or curtains on every window.

Check all the doors. Are they metal or solid wood? Are the frames around the doors secure, or are they loose or broken? If the offender has been ordered out of the home or has moved out, have you changed all the locks? When you change the locks, install a dead bolt and separate peephole on each door.

What about sliding glass doors? This is one of the easiest ways for a person to gain entry to your home. Glass doors can be lifted out from their tracks. Hardware stores sell items like the Club for your home, the Charles Bar, or other devices to keep sliding glass doors from opening. If you can, try to get a good watchdog who will make a lot of noise and draw attention to any trespassers.

Set up an emergency room in your home. Make sure there is a secure lock on the door to the room. Keep a charged portable phone in the room.

When you're not home, use timer switches to turn lights or music on and off. Set your clock radio to go off at various times. Make it appear that you are home. Abusers like the element of surprise. If they believe you or someone else is in the residence, they will probably try to get your attention at another time or place.

It's a good idea to contact your local police department and request their free home safety brochure. Sometimes police departments are willing to send someone to your home free of charge to evaluate your safety and tell you how to safeguard your home.

It is not a good idea to throw out personal information with your regular garbage. You would be surprised how many people go through trash to learn who you are and what you spend. Take your bills, credit cards, banking information, and, yes, even junk mail and dispose of it away from your residence. Sometimes abusers, or the private detectives they hire to track you down, will go through your garbage.

Third, teach your children safety tips. Make sure your child knows how to dial 911. Even if your child isn't able to provide his/her address, operators can usually trace the call to your location. It's a good idea to have your children practice each day on a play telephone with you acting as the operator. Make a game out of it. Ask your child, "What if Mommy couldn't come to the phone, what would you do?" It's also a good idea to practice escape routes with your child. Create a word or signal that will alert your child to trouble. Your child should also be taught that no matter what danger you may be in, the best help he or she can provide in any situation is to go and get help.

CALLER ID

Caller ID enables anyone to view the telephone number of an incoming call on a display unit or telephone set before answering the call. The number is displayed on the caller ID box after the first ring. The caller ID box stores up to one hundred numbers. When you come home you can check to see who has called in your absence. Caller ID can also be turned off so that it will not store numbers. Callers can prevent their numbers from being displayed on someone else's unit by entering a code BEFORE DIALING THE NUMBER. The code is *67 for Touch-Tone phones and 1167 for rotary phones. Phones can be programmed with special equipment to block all calls. Blocking does not affect automatic callback, trap and trace, and call-trace. Blocking will not work from public pay phones. Telephone numbers from pay phones may be dissolved when making local calls. If you have a problem with Caller ID, you can contact your phone company or a domestic violence agency in your area for assistance.

GENERAL TIPS TO HELP YOU STAY SAFE

- Don't release your last name over the phone.
- Don't give out your work address, work phone number, or home address over the phone.
- Try to prevent children from answering the phone, they may not be as wary as an adult.
- Record the dates and times of any harassing calls.

· Whenever you make an outgoing call, dial *67 first. This prevents someone with caller ID from being able to identify your phone number.

· Be warned that dialing *69 enables the person you call to call you back without dialing your number. Therefore, don't place any calls to people who don't know your whereabouts if you think they have this service.

· Contact your local phone company to learn more about what is available for your safety and protection.

making the law work for you

ORDERS OF PROTECTION

An order of protection is a legal step taken by victims of domestic violence and stalking to protect them from someone who is trying to harm them. This order is issued in a court of law before a judge. The purpose of the order is to prohibit the abuser from continuing to be physically violent, harass, stalk, or threaten a particular individual with bodily harm and/or rape. What your court order of protection is called will depend on the state in which you live. Orders of protection can be referred to as: no-contact orders, emergency orders of protection, temporary restraining orders, or simply an order of protection. The type of court order issued to victims of abuse varies from state to state. In most circumstances you do not have to hire a private attorney in order to receive an order of protection.

In order to be better informed on what is available you should contact:

- Your local state's attorney's office

- Your local prosecutor's office

- The attorney general's office

- The local bar association

- Your local battered women's shelter or program

The telephone numbers of the agencies can be found in the yellow pages. All of them provide information on how to obtain orders of protection, whether or not you'll need an attorney, and what costs, if any, are associated with going to court. Because no two cases of abuse are the same, it's important that you explore all of your options before deciding on your best course of action. You can also go to your local library for information on the law and resources available in your state.

POWER OF AN ORDER OF PROTECTION

When you have an order of protection, the court has the power to do the following:

- Give exclusive possession of the residence to the victim (i.e., you).
- Prohibit the abuser from threatening or continuing the abuse.
- Order the abuser to "stay away" from victim's school or workplace.
- Prohibit the abuser from entering the residence if under the influence of drugs or alcohol.
- Recommend or require the abuser to undergo counseling.
- Award possession of personal property to the victim.
- Require temporary support of the victim or their children.
- Require compensation for losses resulting from the abuse.
- Require payment of court costs and attorney's fees.
- Require that the minor children not be taken out of state.
- Place the abuser on an electronic monitoring device.

WHAT AN ORDER OF PROTECTION
CAN AND CANNOT DO

An order of protection is a clear message to the abuser that you intend to end the relationship, but it is no guarantee that the violence will end. Consider your situation very carefully. For some women, securing an order of protection, even if only a temporary one, can be helpful in building a good case against the abuser, perhaps even resulting in jail time for him. In other cases, obtaining an order of protection may only enrage the abuser and encourage him to step up his efforts at harassment or harm. Discuss your circumstances with a domestic violence counselor, trusted friend, or family member who you know will be supportive.

An order of protection is not a bulletproof vest. There's no disputing that fact, since a piece of paper cannot protect anyone from bullets, knives, or fists. However, an order of protection properly enforced by the police, judges, and states' attorneys involved in the process has the power to keep a violent abuser from having the opportunity to engage in further violence. The order of protection gives the legal system and the police an opportunity to act before a tragedy occurs.

Harassment is also prohibited by an order of protection. If your abuser is coming to your home and banging on your door, or if he's constantly calling you on the phone at home or work, this is harassment. If harassment is prohibited by your court order, his behavior constitutes a criminal offense. The police have the right to arrest him for violation of an order of protection. Often a victim of harassment is told by the police that nothing can be done about this behavior. An order of protection gives the police the tools they need to do something.

OBTAINING A CRIMINAL ORDER
OF PROTECTION

To obtain a criminal order of protection you will need a police report of an incident of abuse and the police report case number. There is no cost for the order of protection in criminal court and you are represented in court by the attorney provided by the state in which you reside. The first time you appear in court, the alleged offender will not be present. He will be served with a summons and/or a warrant issued by the judge as you are standing before him in court. The initial order of protection is granted for no more than three weeks. This is called a preliminary, temporary, or emergency order of protection which is kept in place while the state, essentially acting on your behalf, proves its case. Remember, a person (the abuser) is innocent until proven guilty. Regardless of what he has done to you, your abuser must be proven guilty by the state. The abuser has the right to an attorney. If he cannot afford one and provides information to the court that he has little or no income, the court will then appoint a public defender to represent him.

The attorney who is appointed by the state to represent

you will ask you a series of questions. The following are some examples of questions you may be asked when you meet with your attorney:

- Do you have pictures or evidence of your injuries? (They may take pictures at the courthouse.)
- Did you receive medical attention at the time of the alleged abuse? If so, they will ask you for copies of your medical reports.
- Were there any witnesses to the incident?
- Do you have a log or tape of any harassing phone calls?

The attorney asking you these questions is your attorney and is provided free of charge in criminal matters by the state in which you live. He/she needs this information to prepare your case before the judge.

Throughout both the civil and the criminal order of protection process the "petitioner" is the person who is requesting protection for themselves or on behalf of a victim of domestic violence. The "respondent" is the person who has committed abuse and who is being served with the order of protection.

If you and the offender have a child in common and were never legally married, don't be intimidated if he or his attorney asks the court for visitation of the minor child(ren). Usually this is a ploy to see you or further harass you. If parentage has not been determined by a court of law, it should not be an issue for the courts. Even if the abuser's name is on the birth certificate, that does not establish legal parentage. Legal parentage, when the parties are not married, is determined by a blood test after which the court makes its decision. Whatever the case, you must tell the attorney provided to you if you feel that you and your children are in danger.

CIVIL VS. CRIMINAL ORDERS OF PROTECTION

It's important to understand that there are differences between a criminal order of protection and a civil order of protection. For a criminal order of protection to be issued, the abuser has committed a crime against you and he is being charged with that crime. When you obtain a civil order of protection, the abuser has not been charged with a crime. In many situations there just isn't enough evidence for the state to prove a case. Or perhaps the abuser's acts are not considered criminal per the law where you live.

CIVIL ORDERS OF PROTECTION

You petition for a civil order of protection when no criminal charges have been filed against the alleged abuser. Many seek this type of order when they file for divorce. It is still important to obtain pictures for evidence and witnesses just in case your husband's attorney asks for a hearing on the matter. In most cases you are represented by a private or legal aid attorney, not a state's attorney. The procedure for obtaining a civil order of protection varies from state to state, so check with an attorney or a local program for battered women. The order is effective for the same length of time as is the criminal order of protection.

EXTENDING AN ORDER OF PROTECTION

If you feel unsafe when your order is nearing expiration, you can get an extension. To get an extension, you must appear in court on the date and time listed on your document. If you fail to come to court, the order will expire. If you lose your order or it is destroyed, don't panic. Call the court building where you obtained the order and ask for the state's attorney's office or the county clerk's office. They keep copies of these documents on file and will provide you with another copy.

If you absolutely cannot come to court but want your order of protection extended, you must call the state's attorney's office and ask what you should do. They may ask you if there's a medical reason you can't come to court and if so you will need to supply proof of your injury or ailment. They may ask you to complete an affidavit in order to be granted an extension.

HOW TO ENFORCE THE ORDER
OF PROTECTION

If you receive an order of protection, keep a copy with you at all times. It is a crime for your abuser to strike, threaten, or harass you or anyone else named on your order. If your order is violated, call the police immediately and show them a copy of the order. If it is lost or destroyed, tell the police that you have a court order and to please check their computer. Also make sure to do the following:

- If the abuser is present and you want to press charges, tell the police you want the abuser arrested for violating the order (i.e., battery, criminal damage to property, assault, whatever the situation).

- Ask that a police report be filled out and request the report or case number.

- Get the names and badge numbers of the officers who responded to the call.

- If the abuser is not arrested, go back to where you obtained your criminal order of protection and file these new charges as soon as possible after the incident.

- Preserve any evidence (i.e., pictures of injuries and destruction of property or belongings, medical reports, torn or bloodstained clothing, names and addresses of witnesses).

DEFINITIONS OF LEGAL TERMS

Arraignment: The formal act of calling a defendant into open court, informing him of the crime he is charged with, and asking for a plea of guilty or not guilty.

Arrest: The taking of a person into custody for the purpose of holding or detaining him to answer a criminal charge. An arrest can be made when a warrant has been issued or a police officer has reason to believe that an individual has committed a crime.

Bail: An amount of money set by the court, the payment of which allows the release from custody of a person charged with a criminal act. Bail is set in order to ensure that the person charged will appear in court on the date his/her hearing is scheduled and to ensure that the person accused will not violate the conditions of the bond.

Bond: The person accused of a crime binds himself to comply with certain conditions set by the court. The bond is secured by bail or by the signature of the person accused.

Bond forfeiture warrant: If the accused did not appear in court at the proper time, a warrant is issued directing that he be rearrested and that he lose (forfeit) his bond.

Charge: A written statement presented to the court, which accuses a person of committing a crime. A charge can be in the form of a complaint, or, in the case of felonies, an information or indictment.

Complaint: A written statement presented in court charging that a crime has been committed. A complaint can be filed by anyone, including a police officer.

Continuance: When legal proceedings are postponed for a period of time.

Conviction: A finding by a judge or a jury that a person is guilty of a crime based upon evidence or by a guilty plea.

Count: A separate and distinct offense that is included in an indictment or information.

Court reporter: A specially trained stenographer who records the testimony of all parties and the court and later prepares transcripts from the record which may be needed for appeal or review of what took place in court.

Crime: An act committed in violation of the law.

Defendant: The person who has been accused of a crime either by a complaint or an indictment.

Deposition: Testimony taken outside of the courtroom, in writing and under oath. A deposition is not taken in open court, but it is part of the judicial proceeding.

Discovery: This is the process in court and before the judge where the prosecution and the defense supply information about the case to each other.

Dismiss: To end a court action without any further consideration or hearing on the matter.

Disposition: The outcome of the case.

Domestic relations court: A municipal court with jurisdiction over cases involving relations within the family or household, between husband and wife or parent and child.

Domestic violence or abuse: An act of physical violence like slapping, punching, or choking, or harassment or interference with personal liberty by a family or household member, or the intimidation or willful deprivation of a dependent person by a family member or household member. (This does not include reasonable discipline of a minor child by the parent or other person.)

Due process: The regular course of the law throughout the courts of justice. The guarantee of due process is that every person will have the protection of a fair trial under the law.

Evidence: Material and information submitted to the court to be proven or disproved.

Ex parte: A court proceeding brought for the benefit of one side only with no notice to the other side.

Family or household member: Includes spouses, ex-spouses, persons living together, person who formerly lived together, persons related by blood or marriage, parents of a child/stepchildren in common, children, parents, dating-engaged/formerly dating or engaged, person with disability and their personal assistant.

Felony: A major crime such as arson, murder, attempted murder, etc.

Forcible felony: Any felony involving physical force: rape, robbery, burglary, kidnapping, etc.

Guilty: Means that an individual is responsible for a violation of the law.

Harassment: Knowing conduct which is not necessary to accomplish a purpose that is responsible under the circumstances, would cause a reasonable person emotional distress, and does cause emotional distress to the petitioner. The following types of conduct shall be presumed to cause emotional distress: constantly calling the victim's place of work, home, etc.; causing a disturbance at the victim's place of employment; following the victim in public places; keeping the victim under surveillance; threatening to take the victim's children.

Hearsay evidence: Information based on what others have said rather than on a person's own knowledge.

Hung jury: A jury that cannot agree on a verdict.

Incarceration: Being in prison.

Indictment: A written statement presented by the grand jury to a court of law that charges that a crime has been committed. Indictments are brought only in felony cases.

Information: A written statement presented by the grand jury to a court of law which charges that a crime has been committed. Informations are brought only in felony cases.

Interference with personal liberty: Committing or threatening physical abuse, harassment, intimidation, or willful deprivations so as to compel another to engage in conduct from which he/she has a right to abstain or to refrain from conduct in which he/she has a right to engage.

Intimidation: When an individual, with intent to cause another person to perform or omit the performance of any act, communicates to another, whether in person, by telephone, or by mail, either physical confinement or restraint or any other criminal offense.

Mandate: A judicial order directing authorities to enforce a judgment or sentence.

Misdemeanor: A less serious crime than a felony for which imprisonment provided by the law is less than one year.

Mistrial: A trial that is invalidated because of errors in procedure, law, or fact. A new trial before a different jury or judge must be held if a mistrial has been ruled. Mistrials are ruled for failure to reach a verdict, lack of jurisdiction, or errors in the selection of a jury.

Motion to suppress: A request by the defense that certain evidence (such as drugs, guns, clothing, stolen property, confessions) not be used in a trial on the grounds it was not obtained legally.

Notice to appear: A notice issued to a person arrested without a warrant by an officer which sets forth the nature of the crime and requests the accused to appear before a court at a certain time and place.

Objection: A formal challenge that will appear in the court record to material being presented in court. The judge rules on whether the objection is acceptable or not.

Offense: A violation of criminal law.

Perjury: Deliberately testifying falsely under oath.

Physical abuse: Sexual abuse. Knowing or reckless use of physical force, confinement, or restraint. Knowing, repeated, and unnecessary sleep deprivation. Knowing or reckless conduct that creates immediate risk or physical harm.

Plea: The reply of the accused, either guilty or not guilty, to the charges filed against him at the arraignment.

Plea bargaining: Negotiations between the defense and prosecution in which the prosecutor makes concessions regarding the charges and/or sentencing of the accused in exchange for a guilty plea.

Preliminary hearing: After an arrest for a felony the prosecution presents evidence to the judge, who determines whether there is probable cause to believe a crime was committed and the accused may have committed it. If the judge finds probable cause, an information is filed by the prosecutor and the defendant is scheduled for an arraignment.

Probable cause: Circumstances strong enough to lead a prudent person to believe that the party under suspicion may be guilty of a crime.

Probation: A sentence of conditional release under supervision which can be revoked if the conditions are not met.

Reasonable doubt: An actual and substantial doubt arising from a fair comparison and consideration of all the evidence in the case about the guilt of the accused. If a jury has a reasonable doubt about the truth of a charge, then it must render a verdict of not guilty.

Release on recognizance: Bond that is secured by the signature of the person accused. No bail is set.

Rest: A term used when a party has no more evidence to offer at a particular stage of a trial.

Revocation hearing: A hearing in which it is determined whether or not a person sentenced to probation has violated the terms of his probation.

Search warrant: A written order issued by a judge directing law enforcement personnel to search a place or a person for instruments, articles, and things described in the order. In most instances a search warrant must be issued for a search and seizure to be legal.

Sexual assault: When an individual uses force or the threat of force for sexual penetration, commits an act of sexual penetration with the offender knowing that the victim was unable to understand or did not give his/her consent, or commits a sexual act with a minor.

SOL: This is an abbreviation for Stricken Off the Call with Leave to Reinstate. It basically means that the criminal charges are being dropped. If you do not want the charges dropped, be very clear about this when you go before the judge or talk with the prosecutor.

Stalking: Threatening another individual with death, bodily harm, sexual assault, confinement, or restraint by (on more than two separate occasions) following that individual or placing him/her under surveillance by remaining present outside his/her place of employment, car, school, residence. (This law does not apply to picketing at the workplace that arises out of a bona fide labor dispute.)

Aggravated stalking: A person commits aggravated stalking when he/she, in conjunction with committing an offense of stalking, also does any of the following: causes bodily harm, confines, restrains, violates any court order of protection, violates an injunction prohibiting any of these behaviors.

Statute: A section of the Constitution or an act of a state legislature.

Subpoena: A written order calling for an individual's presence in court in a situation involving someone else. A judge or prosecutor usually issues a subpoena.

Supervision: Court order deferring final disposition of a nonfelony case up to two years. If the accused successfully complies with conditions set, charges are dismissed and arrest records may be expunged (wiped off the record).

Summons: Notice issued by the court commanding a person to appear in court at a given time and date. A summons can be sent to an individual charged in a complaint, a witness, or a juror.

Testimony: Statements of witnesses in court under oath.

Threat: When a person communicates the following: physical harm, confinement, restraint, any criminal offense, accusations of a criminal offense, harm to the credit or business reputation of another individual.

Trial: The purpose of a trial, whether it's a bench trial or a jury trial, is to examine evidence, hear testimony, and determine whether the accused is guilty as charged. Like the arraignment, it is a formal public proceeding that is held in a courtroom.

Bench trial: Most misdemeanor trials are bench trials in which a judge rather than a jury renders a verdict. These trials are often very simple, with the judge making a decision after a brief questioning of the accused, complainant, and other witnesses (if any). Occasionally there are bench trials in which defense and prosecuting attorneys find through examination and cross-examination of witnesses.

Jury trial: A panel of twelve individuals is selected to serve as the decision makers in a jury trial. The jury renders the verdict and serves only until the trial is concluded. Anyone accused of a crime has the right to a bench or a jury trial.

Conduct of a trial: The judge is responsible for conducting the trial. Because the jury is required to base its decision only on proper evidence, there is often a dispute between defense and prosecution attorneys as to what is proper (admissible) evidence. The judge must rule on this question as well as on any other points of law that may arise. Usually, he does this by sustaining or overruling an objection by one of the lawyers. But if a question like "When did you stop beating your wife?" is asked, the damage is done and can't be erased. In such an event, attorneys ask to be heard on an objection in the judge's chambers, where they can talk freely without prejudicing the jury. Also during a trial, the jury may be escorted out of the courtroom while defense and prosecution argue points of law before the judge. The judge may take time to advise or instruct the jury on any legal technicalities brought forth in the trial before the jury meets privately to decide on its verdict.

Unlawful restraint: When an individual knowingly, without legal authority, detains another person. (Aggravated unlawful restraint means the use of a weapon.)

Vacate: To cancel or set aside.

Waive: To give up a right, such as the right to a jury or right to an attorney.

Witness: People who have seen an incident or have some information pertaining to the case being tried. Sometimes witnesses are summoned or subpoenaed to appear. Other witnesses volunteer to testify because either the accused or the complainant asks them for help. If you are a witness, you will be asked to tell what you know about the case. You may also be questioned by both the prosecutor and by the defense attorney. Many witnesses want to know how often they will be required to appear in court, but that varies with each case. As a witness, you will be asked to come only when you are required to testify. If you are the complainant, your attorney is the only one who will contact you. In the event he/she is unable to contact you, someone from his/her office will call or notify you by mail in advance to tell you when to be at court. Don't be afraid to call the prosecutor's office if you have any questions or if you are afraid for your safety.

using stalking laws

STALKING AND DOMESTIC VIOLENCE LAWS were passed only after many thousands of women were murdered. When you think about these laws, think about all the women whose lives were brutally taken to make it possible for others to be safe. The majority of stalking laws were passed because the victims' families and friends fought so hard for their passage. One by one those friends and relatives held elected officials accountable for the senseless bloodshed of their daughters, mothers, sisters, children, and friends. The groups who assist battered women have also been silent heroes by helping to draft and fight for laws designed to punish the offenders and protect the victims.

In 1990 California was the first state to make stalking a crime. This landmark legislation led the way for other states to pass similar laws. Now all fifty states have stalking laws.

The majority of the states define stalking as:

- Repeated following

- Harassing behavior

- Willful acts

- Threats

The laws across the country usually require that the victim fear for his or her safety—i.e., bodily harm or fear of death. It is important to know what the laws are in your state and what your rights are. Many states charge an offender with either a misdemeanor (smaller criminal act punishable by law) or a felony (See definitions in Chapter 7). You should also know that the decision as to whether to prosecute a case as a misdemeanor or a felony is the sole responsibility of the state's, or prosecuting, attorney's office. Victims have no input as to what type of crime the offender is charged with.

If the offender is convicted of misdemeanor stalking, he can be sentenced to up to 364 days in jail and given a monetary fine. If an offender is convicted of felony stalking, he can receive three to five years in prison. It is not uncommon for judges to sentence repeat or dangerous stalkers for up to twenty years in prison.

THE CYCLE OF STALKING

The cycle of stalking is very similar to the cycle of domestic violence. Each succeeding act is more terrifying than the previous one. The stalker usually builds through the following steps:

Tension Building Phase

- Phone calls
- Unsolicited letters
- Cryptic "gifts"
- Threats
- Surveillance of the victim
- Following victim
- Minor acts of vandalism
- Increased attempts to control the victim
- Psychological terrorism

If the stalker is unable to get his way by putting the victim completely on edge, he moves on to the:

Explosive or Acutely Violent Phase

- Assault
- Burglary
- Kidnapping
- Violence against victim's family and friends
- Acute acts of vandalism
- Murder/suicide (the perpetrator's final act of control)

Often the stalker will alternate his terrorism tactics with a "hearts-and-flowers phase" (or manipulation). This is simply a new tactic which is sometimes a temporary lapse in stalking. The victim can become complacent about her safety during this period.

This cycle is repeated, escalating in frequency and severity over time. It can continue for years. The perpetrator may move to murder/suicide after the cycle has been repeated several times and it is apparent to the stalker that all of his attempts at coercion have failed. Sometimes the perpetrator abandons his current victim and redirects his fixation to more "challenging" and vulnerable prey—someone who is not yet alert to his dangerous patterns and treachery.

The classification of stalking as a crime is a recent phenomenon, but many local jurisdictions now offer stalking victims protection under their municipal codes, and all fifty states have enacted stalking laws. These laws give enforcement agencies a powerful tool to arrest and prosecute stalkers, offering victims of these terrible crimes much greater protection than ever before.

It is important for people who are being stalked to recognize that this *victimization is not their fault.* Stalking is a crime that can touch anyone, regardless of where they live, with whom they associate, or their economic status. Stalkers vary between those who are a nuisance to those who are violent and intend to do harm. Even though you may think it unlikely that a particular individual will hurt you, *every stalker should be seen as potentially dangerous.*

With increased public attention to the crime of stalking, there are also increased services and resources available for victims of this crime. In addition to becoming familiar with stalking laws that presently exist or are pending in your state and municipality, victims of stalking should be informed about the resources and procedural precautions available to assist and protect them.

If you are in continual danger but no immediate threat (meaning the stalker is on the street corner or circling the block monitoring your activities but has not harmed you in any way), you can make use of restraining/protective/stay-away orders and stalking laws. You should document the activity of the stalker and report his illegal acts to the authorities. You may also seek the assistance of a local battered women's advocate/ crisis counselor. Make contingency plans so that you are not always in the same place at the same time.

The following is a letter which is typical of those we receive from distraught women. It details a typical example of ongoing stalking:

Dear Project:Protect:

I was flipping through the TV stations and ran across a show involving domestic violence. The stories I heard are far too familiar to me. I am writing this letter for ideas and information.

My story is long and I am sure you have heard it all before. I have been divorced for almost three years, my ex-husband STALKS me wherever I seem to go, and the police will do nothing to help me. I've said to many police officers who respond to my calls and then fail to arrest him "Does he have to do bodily harm before you will help me?" And of course I receive no response. I have a restraining order and the police will not enforce it. Their explanation for this is that my claim is just too vague for them to arrest him. You see, he is very clever. He shows up at my home in the middle of the night because he knows he'll be gone by the time the police arrive. He shows up at malls, grocery stores, roller rinks, parks, and any other of a number of places where I or my children happen to be. I have asked the police to write reports for stalking, but they tell me it's my word against his. I even went to the district attorney's office, but they tell me "their hands are tied." I am always searching for ways to protect myself and my children. My ex-husband has threatened to kill me and burn my house down. I fear for the safety of my children. I am afraid someday he will kidnap my children. I am now thinking of relocating to avoid future contact with him. I need your help!

Trapped and Helpless in Oregon

It's very difficult to not be able to live your life in peace. This woman's husband appears to know how to push her buttons, because he's still getting what he wants. Her only response to his stalking is to call the police, and he realizes that in time the police will no longer answer her calls for help. He's waiting for that to happen. In the meantime, he's enjoying aggravating her while he plans his next move.

He has set up a game which he is playing by his own rules. He will continue to play this game until he wins. Winning may cost her and her children their lives. Although she doesn't realize it, the solution is included in her letter. Instead of saying, "I'm thinking of relocating," she should be making plans to move. There is, however, one major hindrance to her relocation, and that is the children. Does she have sole custody of the minor children? Does he have visitation rights? Does he pay child support? She needs to consult with an attorney before making any moves.

She must take extreme care if the courts have granted visitation rights to her ex-spouse. The laws regarding child custody vary from state to state, so it is always important to obtain advice from a lawyer. If the woman has sole custody with no visitation determined by the judge, then she is not bound by a court order to remain in the state. If the offender is paying child support but has no visitation (so she is able to legally leave the state), she should rent a post office box for her mail near her current home so he does not know where she now lives. A trusted family member or friend can pick up the mail and forward it to her. She could also rent a postal box through a private company and have her mail sent there.

I would also advise "Trapped and Helpless in Oregon" to begin to take a family member or friend along with her wherever she goes. A witness can be a great help when she goes to press charges. Until now it has been her word against his. With a witness, the state has the opportunity to prepare a case against her ex-husband, and they have a better chance of getting him convicted of the crime.

She should also consider renting, buying, or borrowing a video camera. This would be a great way to catch him in the act. A video camera will also show the date and time of his appearances, and it can be used in a court of law. A videotape makes a great silent witness.

It is very important for her to seek counseling now. Through counseling, she will find that she is not alone and she can gain the strength she needs to pursue legal remedies against the stalker.

ESCAPING STALKING WHEN
YOU HAVE CHILDREN

If you are married with children, there are special child custody issues to be considered. If you believe that your life and the lives of your children are in danger, *you need to seek the assistance of an attorney in order to remove your children from the situation.* Even when you are a victim of abuse, in some states you can be charged with child endangerment, or even lose custody of your children, because you failed to remove them from a dangerous environment. On the other hand, unless you follow proper legal channels, you can be charged with kidnapping if you take your children out of state. That is why *documentation is vital to your case.* It's important to realize that no matter what an offender has done or how abusive he has been to you, the courts usually do not deny him visitation privileges or strip him of his parental rights. Leaving an abusive relationship is decidedly easier when you are childless. Be aware that all states have child abduction laws and many offenders will try to turn around a situation if you haven't made police reports or filed for an order of protection or sought medical assistance for injuries you received because you were battered. That's why documentation is so important when it comes to removing the children from the home. If no documentation exists, seek the help of a lawyer, or else the offender can use the child abduction or kidnapping laws against you.

STALKING WITH LETTERS AND NOTES

Stalking is not just a matter of being followed or called on the telephone, nor can you feel completely safe even when he's been locked up. On those too-few occasions when offenders have been convicted of abuse and are incarcerated, they often write letters from prison to the women they've abused. We've reviewed many cases across the country where offenders send "love" letters to those they tried to harm. *It is important to recognize that these letters are another form of intimidation and harassment. It's the stalker's way of letting you know that he will be back.* By sending you letters, the offender is sending you a clear message of veiled threats that only you can understand or decode. If you have a court order that prohibits contact of any kind by this person, get in touch with the prosecuting attorney immediately and let him know that your order of protection has been violated. Just because the offender is in jail does not mean that he can't be brought back into court and charged and tried for violating your order of protection. In some cases the offender will receive additional jail time.

DAWN AND CHRISTOPHER WILSON

Dawn and Christopher Wilson were married on July 29, 1988, and the following year Dawn gave birth to a baby girl. The marriage had its ups and downs, in fact more downs than ups. After the birth of their child, Christopher grew more violent. His temper and use of physical force became routine. Dawn realized this was no way to live. In November 1989 she filed for divorce. And on March 1, 1990, the divorce was final.

Christopher used the child visitation granted by the divorce court as justification to continue his violence. As far as he was concerned, Dawn and his daughter, divorce or not, still belonged to him. Christopher didn't care about the child; he used his visitation time to verbally and physically assault Dawn.

On June 10, 1991, while on a visit with his daughter, Christopher dragged Dawn from her apartment by her hair and pulled her into the alleyway. His intention was to beat her to death, and he almost succeeded. Fortunately, a young couple heard Dawn's screams for help and came to her rescue. The injuries Dawn sustained were severe and life-threatening. Her face was so unrecognizable that she's had four reconstructive surgeries to repair the damage.

Six weeks later Christopher was captured, tried, and sentenced to three years at a state correctional facility. Dawn thought her nightmare had finally ended. Then Christopher began calling and sending her letters from prison. In his letters he made a number of threats including: "You'll never keep me from her" (meaning their daughter) and that he would "try and do anything (I mean anything) to get information on what my daughter is doing and what she looks like and if she is happy." In other letters he made statements like "They can't keep us apart" (written to his daughter, who is too young to read) and "Why do you act like you're the victim and I'm the criminal" and "You're gonna have to deal with me in life sometime down the road."

In April 1992 Dawn Wilson testified before the Illinois House Judiciary Committee during the hearings on the stalking bill which became law in Illinois on July 12, 1992. She made the following statement:

> *My name is Dawn Wilson. I was married to a man for one and a half years, who I divorced for constant physical abuse. He has since constantly followed me and*

threatened me. Following my divorce, he has been arrested nine times for battery, violation of protective orders, and forcible entry to my apartment.

Finally on June 10, 1991, after being informed by law enforcement officials and our court system that their hands were tied as to what they could do to help, I was severely beaten by this man. If not for other citizens who responded to my screams for help, I too would be dead.

I have no doubt that when my ex-husband is released he will kill me. I do not want to die. I do not want my daughter Christi to grow up without her mother.

On October 21, 1992, Dawn's attorney, myself, and Dawn were able to get Christopher arrested immediately following his release from prison for writing letters, an action prohibited by Dawn's order of protection. We were helped by the Chicago media, whose coverage of Dawn's story put the needed pressure on the judicial system. Throughout the next several months, while Christopher was awaiting trial, we continued to put pressure on the legal system by appearing not only on local TV but also on national television shows. For each media appearance we brought the pictures that told the story of the brutal beating Dawn had suffered. Because of our efforts and the media's attention, Christopher spent an additional ten months in jail. We were also able to have Christopher's parental rights revoked. Dawn then adopted her daughter, a legal maneuver that ensured that Christopher could never reclaim the child.

Dawn and her daughter were finally free of Christopher.

In December 1994 I received a telephone call from the Illinois State Police. Christopher Wilson was at it again. This time he had a new victim and was repeating the same violent behavior in his new relationship. Because of the attention focused on the original case, the police stepped up their efforts to arrest him. They began a massive manhunt for his capture and within forty-eight hours they had him in custody. Today Christopher is in jail, where he will be for a very long time.

Although it may appear that Dawn and her daughter can now peacefully resume their lives, that is only wishful thinking. Dawn will always live with the memories of that brutal night and her fight for safety and justice. We made a promise to each other when we began. If she survives, then I must promise to continue to assist others like her. It's one promise I am happy to honor.

how friends and family
can help

ONE OF THE REASONS my mother remained with my father for so many years was that she had no encouragement from her family to leave him. Instead of encouraging her and helping her to leave, my mother's family consistently told her that if she changed her behavior, my father's abuse would stop. My mother made every effort to follow their advice. It didn't work.

WHAT CAN I DO TO HELP?
WHERE DO I START?

I lived with my daughter and granddaughter for almost a year. My daughter was stalked by her ex-husband. He would wait for her at her place of work or around her apartment. Often she would come home and tell me that he was outside the window and, again, we would call the police. Eventually he kicked the door in, cutting the top of my foot to the bone with a butcher knife and he beat my daughter while she was holding their daughter to protect her child from any blows. He fled the scene before the police arrived. Then he called me and stated that "this was just the beginning." I was able to keep him on the phone and learn his whereabouts. Eight hours later he was picked up by the police. He was held without bond and sentenced to one year in jail for violation of probation (spousal abuse). The judge also gave him a year's probation and told him he was to have no contact with his ex-wife or any member of her family.

While he was in jail my daughter and I moved, with the assistance of the police department, and relocated out of state. With the help of law enforcement, we changed the addresses on our driver's licenses, car registrations, and all other information to a post office box.

Within 24 hours of his release, my daughter's ex-husband began trying to locate her. He called her former place of employment and demanded to speak to his "wife" and to be told where she had gone. Although it's been two years and my daughter is remarried and is expecting a child, she still reacts every time his name is mentioned. Although he has returned to his family in Kentucky, he still calls my oldest daughter (his ex–sister-in-law) and demands to know where his "wife" is living. Everyone who knows him feels that one day he will find my daughter.

Because we are a large and strong family, we will con-tinue to do everything in our power to ensure that this won't happen. I realize this letter is long, but if there is something I can do to help just one woman in this terrible type of situation, I would. Until you have walked that mile in the shoes of the stalked, there is no way to understand the fear.

As I read this letter, I realized how lucky this daughter is to have such a strong and supportive family. They weathered the storm as a team. In many situations women do not have family members who are willing to see them through to safety. Sometimes a woman has no family, or the abuser has isolated her from her family, or her family is also abusive and does not see his abuse as a serious or life-threatening problem.

The writer of this letter asked how she could help others. A good starting point would be for her to contact a local shelter and volunteer her time. Most battered women's agencies across the county have limited staff and resources and welcome volun-teers. A few hours of your time each week can be very useful to an agency.

HOW YOU CAN HELP

If you see any of these signs or behavioral patterns in a loved one or friend, you should not look away. There is probably abuse in the house if she:

- Cannot do anything without checking with her partner.
- Has become quiet or unusually withdrawn (doesn't act like the same person).
- Seldom has any cash and is always making excuses about forgetting money.
- Wears concealing clothing even in hot weather.
- Has a bruise on a different area of her body every time you see her.
- Is suddenly "accident prone."
- Has been calling in sick to work a lot.
- Never comes to family dinners or gatherings.
- Constantly looks fatigued or under a lot of stress.
- Can't stay on the phone when you call.
- Snaps at you or others for no reason at all.
- Has stopped seeing her close friends.
- Never invites anyone over.

The most important thing you can do for a friend or family member who is being abused is to let the person know you care. She needs to know that you are there for her, no matter what.

If someone reaches out to you for help, don't ignore her and don't pass off the incident of abuse as an accident. Abuse is against the law; these are not accidents, they are crimes. If you choose to ignore her appeals for help, she could be killed. Listen to the person who comes to you for assistance or advice. Do not judge her and do not minimize the extent of what she says is going on.

We teach our children to stay away from strangers. We teach grown women never to park their vehicles in dark places or to pull over for a stranded motorist. We teach awareness of AIDS, drugs, and alcohol, but we consistently fail to warn about domestic violence or teach safe relationship techniques.

If you have a friend or relative whom you think is being abused, *do some research on the issue of abuse.* Go to the library or contact a local agency for women who have been abused. Find out what the agencies do to provide support.

First and foremost, be supportive. If your friend or family member tells you about her abusive partner:

- Embrace her, don't turn away.

- Don't underestimate the situation.

- Believe her. Don't say "That's impossible" or "I find what you're telling me hard to believe."

- Offer information or suggestions on women's agencies who can help her.

- Don't talk about the wonderful qualities the abuser appears to have. It's obvious from what she's saying that you don't know him as well as you think.

- Express your concern for her safety.

- Offer to assist her with a safety plan.

Remember that the abuser expects his affable behavior to fool you into believing him rather than the victim. You need to realize that most abusers are capable of presenting themselves as two completely different people. Outside their homes, they appear to be wonderful fathers, husbands, providers, men who are always there to lend a helping hand. If you want to be supportive to the woman who is being abused, you have to realize that the abusive person is really two different people. The abuser is a great manipulator and is clever about hiding his true emotions. He wants you to believe that the victim is not telling the truth.

One of the things an abuser counts on most is that his victim will be too terrified to disclose the incidents of verbal and/or physical abuse. If the abuser learns that the victim has confided in you, he may deny the truth of her allegations, or he may provide explanations like:

- She's making too much of this.

- She's under severe emotional stress right now.

- She's just trying to get your attention.

- She just hasn't been herself lately. I've tried to get

her to seek professional help, but she just won't listen.

· You've known me for a long time, do you actually believe I could be capable of being abusive toward her or anyone?

· She's going through the change of life.

· I just blew up one time, I didn't mean to do it.

· We're having a few problems, but it's nothing we can't work out.

· This is a family matter. Mind your own business.

· I'd had a little too much to drink (or was using some other substance).

It is extremely important that you do not judge the person who is disclosing the abuse.

· Don't blame her for the abuse.

· Don't suggest that it is just her imagination or that she should try to be a better wife.

· Listen very carefully to what she is telling you.

· Don't jump to any conclusions.

· Validate her feelings by focusing on her strengths as a person.

· Suggest ways for her to get help.

· If she wants to leave, be supportive and offer some suggestions or strategies for leaving.

- Let her use your phone to gather information; it may not be safe for her to call anyone from her home, the abuser may be receiving monthly records of calls placed from their phone.

- Make a list of people she can call in an emergency and keep a copy.

- Allow her to keep items for her escape at your house.

- Come up with alternatives for temporary housing because the domestic violence agency may be full.

- Create an easy code word or signal for her to use in the event she's in immediate danger.

- If she has to appear in court or sign a complaint at the police station, go with her; don't let her go alone.

WHAT SHOULD I DO IF I SUSPECT A FRIEND OR RELATIVE IS BEING ABUSED?

Asking someone you know or love about potential abuse can be very difficult. Before confronting your friend or loved one, think about what you will say first. It's easy for all of us to look at the situation from the outside and know what to do. However, when a person who you love and care about is on the inside, she can't always see what's happening to her. You will have trouble if you begin your conversation by judging her and saying things like:

- You're crazy to stay with him.
- Don't you care about the children?
- Just get out, pack your bags, and leave.
- How can you still be in love with him?
- What's happened to you? Where's the person I used to know?

Before you approach this delicate subject with a friend or family member, you should realize that this person has been told by someone who is supposed to care, support, and love her that she is ugly, incompetent, mentally ill, and/or just plain useless. She may think this is all her fault. She usually has a strong emotional attachment to her partner. Many times the victim feels the abuse is a reflection on her because she chose her husband. She may think that she should have known better. If she tries to confide in anyone or leave, she may feel that it means she's not a very good judge of character. She has learned to take the responsibility for his behavior over the course of their relationship and believes that she is the cause of the abuse. Maybe she believes that she just won't make it emotionally or financially without this person. She may confide in you and say "But I've tried to leave and he's always stopped me." She may fear for her safety or that of her children. She may think that staying is the solution to her problem.

You should also realize that the abuser doesn't hurt her

just because he drinks or does drugs. His abusive behavior is learned. Sometime during his childhood he may have witnessed his father treating his mother the same way. He thinks his behavior is normal or at least that it is a way to keep order and control in the family. If you think of the abuser as a "sick person," you are just excusing him from taking responsibility for his behavior. The abuser knows exactly what he is doing and he will continue to act this way because he is able to get away with this behavior.

Approach the subject of abuse in a nonconfrontational way. Perhaps you saw a movie or a documentary that recently ran on television. Tell her you didn't realize how widespread the problem was and that you are concerned about anyone who is forced to live under those conditions. You could also check the yellow pages of your phone book for women's shelters, crisis intervention centers, and battered women's agencies and ask for information about their programs. Make sure they send you some of their literature. Once you've received the information, invite your friend or relative over for coffee and leave the material sitting on the table. You can say that one of your kids is doing a report on domestic violence or that you are thinking about volunteering time to a shelter and what does she think. Encourage her to look over the information and try to have a conversation. Encourage her to call service providers who deal with victims of abuse. Tell her that the services are free and confidential. Let her know that you are there at any time to listen to her and support her. Tell her that you care about her very much.

If both the victim and the abuser are your friends or relatives, recognize that the victim is trusting you and honor that trust. Don't disclose what she's told you to the offender or get his side of the story. Chances are the person who is being abusive will not be honest with you. By talking with the abuser, you may be exposing the victim to even greater danger. Her abuser could decide to attack her just because she confided in you. If you feel that you must talk to the offender, be sure to ask the victim how she feels about your talking to him.

Make sure to offer some type of assistance. Don't act as though there is nothing you can do. Don't think the situation will disappear or work itself out. Recognize that part of the reason he is abusive is that he can get away with it. Understand that she has lost all of her confidence. That she is not the same person she once was. As a friend or relative, you need to be aware that she is the victim of a crime that could result in further injury or possible death. Understand that if there are children involved, they could also be in harm's way.

Sit down with her in a safe, private place, somewhere where you and she will be comfortable. Suggest that she begin to think about leaving. Have pen and paper ready. Begin to briefly outline ways to get out. Let her know that you are there to help and support her in whatever decision she makes. If there are children involved, try to explain that living with this abuse is only preparing the children to repeat the cycle of violence and that she has the ability to break this cycle.

In the appendixes of this book are names, addresses, and

telephone numbers of programs and agencies who assist victims of domestic violence. They are arranged alphabetically and by state, then by city within the state. The list can get you started in providing assistance to a friend or relative who is being abused.

■

TEN

what we still need to do

Dear Project:Protect,

I am writing because I need help. I am not a physically abused wife, my husband is mentally abusive and has a very bad temper. I want to be prepared if he ever goes after me instead of punching holes in our walls. Sometimes I am afraid to go home at night because I don't know what kind of mood he will be in. I have to tiptoe around and be very careful. I don't want to say the wrong thing or he'll blow up.

I know I probably sound like an idiot for not leaving him, but I can't. I know if I try to leave, he'll come after me, and find me, no matter whom I run to. I think of different ways out every day, and nothing seems solid enough.

My husband is now thinking about buying a gun, and it scares me to death to even think about it. He swears he would never even think about using it on me, but I don't want to take a risk. A man with his temper and instability is capable of doing anything.

Please send me as much information as you can about making a plan to leave, and any other information you think will help.

Someday, with a solid plan, I will get out of here.

Thank you,

Joan

This letter shows how hopeless a battered woman can feel. Joan begins by minimizing her situation, but then, as she continues to write, she expresses her terror. She apparently does not believe in herself. She calls herself an idiot and distrusts her own desire to leave. Joan's willingness to write and ask for help is an indication of her desperation and isolation. There are hundreds of thousands of women like Joan who need our help.

WHAT CAN YOU DO TO HELP?

You can begin by contacting your local domestic violence agency. Programs that assist victims provide a wide range of services, and they are always in need of volunteers. You could volunteer for:

- A crisis line—usually staffed twenty-four hours a day for counseling, shelter intervention, information, and referrals.

- A shelter—most agencies offer training to those wishing to volunteer. They provide temporary housing for abused women and their children. A warm, caring, friendly face can make a difference to these victims who are faced with having to flee, often with nothing more than the clothes on their backs. You could offer to read to children, obtain leads for jobs or housing, and the like.

- Participate in fund-raising activities—many programs are not able to rely on the grant money they receive and rely on the general public for support. You could offer to host a fund-raising activity or volunteer your time to raise money. If you have a special talent for writing, speaking, computers, organization, or special contacts, you could offer your services. You could offer to arrange a presentation at your place of employment or offer to assist in the office with clerical work, mailings, telephone calls, scheduling, etc. If you are an attorney or physician, you can offer to assist women in the legal process, or provide medical assistance. You could coordinate letter-writing campaigns to officials about changes relating to problems to victims of abuse.

MAKING A DIFFERENCE

Since 1990, when I began my work protecting families, I have often been discouraged by the lack of support for changing public attitudes toward violent abuse in the home. If you think the cost of violence doesn't affect each and every American across the United States, you are very much mistaken. If you think your voice doesn't have any impact, you are wrong—it does. When you vote, elect people who will actually be the voice of the people. We can't continue to sit back watching and waiting for a miracle to happen; life doesn't work like that. Everybody must get involved and be a member of the team that puts an end to domestic violence. There is great strength in numbers, and if enough Americans come together and work for change, those we have placed in office will have no choice but to listen to "we, the people."

I am asking you to write to the elected officials who represent you in Congress, and to your state legislature. Do this not just for us adults, but especially for the effect it will have on our children! Personal letters from those who live in the area that a legislator represents take only a few minutes to write and send, and can be very effective in gaining support for a position or program. Taking time to make your voice heard is crucial!

TIPS ON WRITING LETTERS TO
ELECTED OFFICIALS

1.   Address: *U.S. House of Representatives:* You do not need a specific building or room number. Using your representative's name, you can send letters to the United States House of Representatives, Washington, DC 20515. If you don't know the name of your representative, call the public library to obtain that information, and the addresses of your state legislators.

U.S. Senate: Address your letter to each of the two senators for your state, and send them to: U.S. Senate, Washington, DC 20510. Be sure to include your home address on all correspondence.

2.   Be specific. When you write, relate the benefits of the program you are writing about. Enclose articles or fact sheets on the program. Use examples of how you, your children, a relative, neighbor, or your community can specifically benefit from what you are requesting. Write to tell them why a particular program should receive an increase in funding, or if there are plans for the program to be cut, why it should remain intact. Use names when you refer to individuals. It is also a good idea to ask others in your community to send letters. Your church can be a strong voice; ask church officials and members to get involved.

3.   Personal letters only. Do not use form letters, copies of letters, carbons, or post cards. Write to each elected official

individually, or the credibility of your effort will be reduced. Handwritten letters are fine, as long as they are easy to read.

4. One issue per letter. Keep your letter clearly focused on one issue. State your position directly and request the policymaker's support.

5. Use examples. It is helpful to back up your position with any current reliable numbers that directly relate to your issue. It is important to realize that personal experience is just as valuable as research data. For example, use sentences such as "When I was looking for child care, the only center within thirty minutes of my home had a waiting list of sixty children." Do not use information or statistics you are not sure of.

6. Technicalities. Do not be intimidated by the technicalities of the legislative process. Think about it for a moment; were the legislators shy when they asked for your vote so they could be elected? Absolutely not! If you can specifically name the program—head start, violence prevention, prisons, electronic monitoring, block grant funding, schools, funding cuts, etc.—and define your concern, you will be more effective. It is helpful if you know the numbers of related bills or their sponsors, but not crucial.

7. Write early and often. Let your legislator know you care about a program before it is on the chopping block or on the front page of your local newspaper, and before she/he is committed to a position you may not like! When your legislator speaks or votes in support of your program, write a note of thanks. When she/he speaks or votes against your program, write to offer information that might alter his/her position the next time. For example, "I understand you voted to reduce funding. In the future, will you please consider that many children are benefiting from this program. After school, it keeps them from harm and the gangs."

8.   **Share.** Make copies of your letter and share it with others, such as the director of the program you are writing about and people in your community. When you encourage them to write similar letters, it is much easier if they have a letter to use as a model. It might be a good idea to form small groups to track specific issues.

9.   **Courtesy is persuasive.** To be most effective on behalf of a program or concern, always use a respectful and courteous tone rather than a righteous or angry one. Even if you disagree with the legislator's past actions and positions, stress the positive. For example, "I am confident that you will lend your valuable support to this needed program."

10.   **DO IT AND MAIL IT!** It does not have to be great literature; what is important is to help your legislator understand how your program affects real people like you.

For further information, Project:Protect has a national newsletter: *Voices for Change Across America.* For a subscription, send your name, address, city, state, zip code, and telephone number (optional) with a check or money order ($60 each year) to: Project:Protect, P.O. Box 31124, Chicago, IL 60631. Subscriptions are available only by mail. Please do not try to order by telephone. Proceeds from the sale of the newsletter go directly to support various programs for women who are escaping abusive situations: housing, toll-free help-lines, protective agencies, advocacy services, relocation, and transportation. The newsletter covers issues and concerns relating to domestic violence all across the country. It also monitors legislative activity, and insists that those we elect to office not only listen, but respond.

SHELTERS

First of all, there are not enough shelters. The few that are available lack resources and bed space. Agencies across the country, because they lack sufficient funding and community support, are forced to turn away four out of every five women who call for assistance. Additionally, while a shelter provides a temporary safe haven, it does nothing to resolve the basic problem. We need shelter programs that respond to long-term needs and that offer a full range of services to assist women who are fleeing their abusive relationships to move on with their lives.

An ideal program would include the following:

· Housing services for up to two years

· Training and job placement

· Full legal services

- A voucher program so the women can return to school
- Emergency assistance on a short-term basis
- Comprehensive victim-witness services that include court advocacy
- Counseling programs for women and their children

RAISING COMMUNITY AWARENESS ABOUT STALKING AND DOMESTIC VIOLENCE

To create a climate in your community that is supportive of women who are victims of domestic violence, accumulate materials and information on community agencies and their leaders, including:

- School personnel
- Church officials
- Social service agencies
- Programs for women who have been abused
- Local hospitals

Contact these agencies and find out what services they have for victims of domestic violence. After you have identified the community leadership at the agencies, get suggestions on key individuals from each agency to form an active working group.

Set objectives and plan strategies focusing on matching local resources with community needs. Organize stalking presentations (i.e., offer statistics, scoreboard examples, newspaper/magazine articles providing proof of need). Provide handouts from your local women's agencies and other service providers. Provide names and telephone numbers of law enforcement and legal service agencies in your community.

SUCCESSFUL MEDIA STRATEGIES

Inform other law enforcement officers of the formation of your select community leadership committee (list key committee leadership) through in-house law enforcement newsletters. Inform public officials of the formation of this law enforcement/community leadership committee on stalking. Encourage organizations to publish this information in their newsletters. Plan activities like a law enforcement/open community forum and invite public officials and all executive personnel of schools, churches, social service agencies, women's agencies, stalking programs, local hospital officials, and other pertinent law enforcement officials.

Send well-written articles that include the information listed in the newsletter to local newspapers, stating the date, time, and place of your forum. Inform television and radio stations of the event by delivering the press article to them.

Appoint someone with a media or public relations background to handle follow-up phone calls. Know that proper media strategy is imperative to the success of your forum. Rely on the power of your presentation to draw media attention.

On the day of the forum, hold a press conference with top public officers, committee members, etc., just prior to the opening of the community forum. For the press conference, select a site that is identified with domestic violence and stalking. Invite top officials such as the mayor, police chief, congressional representative, or president of the school board to speak at the press conference to demonstrate their support. Be sure to involve representatives from groups who work with battered women.

The more local information you have on stalking and domestic violence, the more media attention you will get. Prepare a fact sheet to give to reporters on this issue. Contact local radio talk shows to promote the event, and inform listeners about this new initiative.

RELOCATION PROGRAMS

Possibly the largest problem Project:Protect faces is ensuring the total safety of the women who come to us by relocating them. Many women have great difficulty relocating themselves. Because of the sophistication of contemporary technology, it is not very easy to disappear, especially if the person looking for you has an intimate knowledge of your habits. We encourage victims of domestic violence to leave, make them jump through hoops to remain safe, yet we provide little if any real resources to ensure their safety. Women must be given a chance to stay alive.

To keep them safe, we need to act as if the victim is in the Federal Witness Protection Program. We need to implement a program that provides the following services:

- Complete change of name for the woman and her children
- New social security numbers
- New school records
- New medical record information
- New birth certificates
- New driver's licenses

New identity relocation programs such as this are not required in every situation, but should be available in certain cases. Any person requesting this type of relocation needs to understand that she can never contact her friends or family members again, and she will be required to move to a new state. Such a program needs to be put in place at the national level, and would indeed save lives.

To implement this plan, or any other, we must actively engage every level of our community and every person in our society. It will require a focus on a coordinated action, cooperative strategies, collaboration of principal parties within our system, and enhanced communication on all levels. We must strengthen the link between the system and the people, educate citizens and mobilize massive media campaigns to implement programs that enable victims to live their lives safely and productively.

ELECTRONIC MONITORING PROGRAM

Victims of stalkers, batterers, and sex offenders feel they are prisoners in their own homes, afraid to go out in public, where their attacker could be waiting behind a bush, in a car, or just around the corner, ready to strike without warning.

An electronic monitoring system has recently been developed specifically to help protect victims of ongoing criminal assault. The system offers protection to victims while also monitoring the offender. The offender wears a tamper-sensitive ankle transmitter that communicates through a receiver in his home to a central monitoring center. The victim also gets a receiver in her home which sends a signal if the offender comes within range of her. When the signal is received by the monitoring center, the police are contacted, and the victim is also notified. In addition, the victim receives a pager so she can be contacted if she is away from home. The victim is also given a backup emergency pendant that emits a signal in case the offender confronts her. When the signal is received at the monitoring center, the police are immediately notified that a "life-threatening" situation is in progress.

At the moment, when stalking/domestic violence crimes

are reported, the police take action, but eventually the offender is out on the street again. Fewer than half the inmates incarcerated in state prisons have been convicted of violent crimes, and of that group, most serve approximately one-third of their sentences. For example, the California prison system is at 188 percent capacity, costing the state 2.4 billion dollars a year. Overcrowding alone can explain why offenders are shortly returned to the community after committing family violence crimes. What then? Will it happen again? When? Where? A court-issued protection order does not stop these attacks from recurring, and it may take only one more attack for the victim to be seriously hurt or killed. An electronic monitoring system will by no means stop a bullet. It is, however, an alternative by which law enforcement can monitor an offender's activities.

Victims also need better protection in the court system. When offenders are released without the court keeping some sort of control and accountability for their activities, they are free to strike again. I have researched electronic monitoring equipment and I believe it can save lives and cost far less than placing the offender behind bars. To receive information on this system, please write to Project:Protect.

DOMESTIC VIOLENCE UNITS

Currently, with the exception of the Los Angeles Threat Management Unit, there are no real domestic violence units within police departments. Most departments have divisions for violent crimes, sexual assault, robbery, gang crimes, etc., but no specific unit dealing with this common and escalating problem. If such units existed, police departments and local governments would see a real change in the number of stalking and domestic violence crimes.

CRIME REPORTING CATEGORY

We have a crime reporting category for murder, rape, robbery, carjacking. Throughout the year, reports are generated on the number of people who are affected by specified crimes, and then, in turn, that information is broken down into categories. We do not, however, have such a system for victims of domestic violence, who are abused, stalked, murdered each year because of that abuse. These crimes go unreported, or they are lumped with other crime categories.

We know how many people die each year as a result of drunk driving. Because this crime has its own category, the public at large responds to this very serious problem more effectively. The same must be done for victims of abuse. A separate crime reporting category will let society know how costly and dangerous abuse is, and how it affects us all. Creating and maintaining a crime category will hold the system accountable and encourage the government to take more steps to ensure the safety of women and children across the country.

FIREARM REVOCATION

There are a lot of offenders who keep weapons either legally or illegally in the home. Every state needs laws mandating the removal of all firearms from the home pending the outcome of the offender's case. If the person is found not guilty of the crime, then the weapons can be returned. If, however, the accused is found guilty of the offense, his firearm card must be terminated, and all his weapons confiscated.

NATIONAL COMPUTER REGISTRY

All too often the system is not equipped with information on an alleged offender involving domestic violence or stalking crimes. We have, in fact, had situations where the victim had no real knowledge of the person with whom she had entered into a relationship. In one situation, a woman began a relationship with a man who had been wanted in another state for murder. She ultimately was shot five times and remarkably survived. The man was able to create a new life by changing his name. We learned who he really was only after the crime was committed. There are too many of these cases, and a registry would assist everyone.

WORKPLACE VIOLENCE

It is a sad reality that many victims of abuse or stalking lose their jobs every year, either because they missed too many days of work, or because they were constantly being stalked and called at the workplace. California has legislation that should be part of federal law. In California, employers are able to file charges on behalf of the workplace or the employee(s) who is being harassed or stalked. In addition, more corporations need to have employee assistance programs that not only ensure safety, but stand behind valuable employees who need their support.

MARRIAGE LICENSE FEES

Some states have implemented a one-dollar surcharge on every marriage license issued in the state to fund programs that combat domestic violence. I do not think that is enough. I would like to see a $5 charge attached to every marriage license issued in every state. The money could fund the comprehensive approach outlined above, and could include relocation services.

VICTIM NOTIFICATION

When offenders are released from prison, or have made bail, it is crucial that their victims be notified immediately. In many cases, the victim is totally unaware that her abuser is no longer locked up; not being on her guard, she tragically loses her life. We need a federal law that requires notification to victims no matter where they reside. We also need stiffer penalties for crimes committed by an offender while he is out on bail.

DOMESTIC RELATIONS COURT

Judges who oversee civil cases in which women obtain divorces are doing a great disservice to victims of abuse. Judges are not educated about the danger of intimidation, threats, stalking, surveillance, or the risk of violence that leads to the woman's sense of helplessness. When judges advise and pressure women who are suffering from abuse to settle, get along with, or trust their spouses, they are encouraging the offenders to continue their behavior. The courts must learn the patterns and characteristics of spousal abuse and abusers.

In cases of child custody, offenders are very aware of how to use child visitation and custody as a "club" with which to control women. Without supporting evidence, little attention is paid to a woman's testimony regarding her abuser's use of alcohol and drugs, his behavior and/or threats. This type of controlling, manipulative behavior is not in the best interests of the children, and as a matter of fact is often considered child endangerment.

In situations where a woman has little or no income, she is at a real disadvantage in disputes over protective orders and child custody. The economically disadvantaged party is often *forced* to agree to an unfair settlement, perhaps even putting the divorce at risk if she does not comply. For many women who are unable to pay legal fees, it is extremely difficult to be awarded attorney's fees and interim fees in the divorce settlement. This has a definite effect on the woman's ability to obtain competent legal representation. What judges are not seeing is that this is a very real problem, and it must be addressed in all divorce cases in which abuse is or has occurred.

EQUAL ACCESS FOR ALL WITHOUT DISCRIMINATION

Abuse is about power and control. People with disabilities often do not have the same rights as those who are not disabled. In many cities across the country there are access ramps to, or special equipment at, police stations, courthouses, schools, public health centers, banks, public transportation, etc. A victim of abuse is further victimized when the system does not make access to these places possible for her. It is my hope that we advocate for the right of the disabled community to have the same services and use of those services that the rest of us enjoy and take for granted.

The work Project:Protect does to protect the rights of women and their children is extensive. The job of our agency would be easier if everyone understood that domestic violence and stalking are crimes, not misunderstandings. It would also help if there were not only additional services available, but if these services were tailored to the individual victim and her family. I pride myself on keeping a woman and her children safe and not operating a program that temporarily shields them and then sends them back out to their doom. We are engaged in a war, and although we may win a few battles, we cannot have a victory without a plan of action.

We need a more comprehensive approach to dealing with this issue. We can no longer put a bandage on these women's wounds and send them on their way. It is my hope that you will join us in creating changes that in the long run will save not only money—because crime reaches into every American's pocket—but lives.

I have compiled a list of programs that Project:Protect sees as necessary to keep everyone that we assist safe (See appendixes). Perhaps you can find out if such programs exist in your area, and if they do not, we would like your assistance in getting them started.

■

In conclusion, the only words I can think of are the ones I use every time I finish speaking at a luncheon, dinner, or workshop—they have become my signature. When one life is lost, we all lose.

national directory of domestic violence programs by state

(Sign language is listed as ASL, i.e. American Sign Language)

ALABAMA

Family Violence Center
Birmingham
(205) 322-4878
(205) 521-9646

Safeplace, Inc.
Florence
(205) 767-6210
(205) 767-3076
French, German, Spanish

HOPE Place, Inc.
Huntsville
(205) 539-1000
(205) 534-4052
Interpreters available

ALASKA

Abused Women's Aid Crisis
(AWAIC)
Anchorage
(907) 272-0100
(907) 279-9581
In-house Spanish referrals

Arctic Women in Crisis (AWIC)
Barrow
(800) 478-0267
(907) 852-0267
Inupiaq, Chinese, Tagalog

Women in Crisis—Counseling
& Assistance
Fairbanks
(800) 478-7273
(907) 452-2293
(907) 452-6770
Spanish, contact deaf interpreters

Advocates for Victims of
Violence (AVV)
Valdez
(907) 835-2999
(907) 835-2980
*Spanish, German, Korean, Thai,
Chinese*

ARIZONA

Tri Community Counseling Safe
Home Network
Oracle
(800) 362-3474
(602) 896-9240
Spanish

Time Out Domestic Violence
Shelter
Payson
(800) 294-9025
(602) 472-8007
Spanish

Tucson Centers for Women &
Children
Tucson
(602) 795-4880
(602) 795-8001
(602) 795-4266
Spanish

ARKANSAS

Abused Women and Children,
Inc.
Arkadelphia
(501) 246-2587
(501) 246-3122

Advocates for Battered Women
Little Rock
(800) 332-4443
(500) 376-3219

Domestic Violence Prevention
Texarkana
(800) 876-4808
(903) 793-4357
(903) 794-4000
Spanish

CALIFORNIA

North County Women's
Resource Center
Atascadero
(800) 549-8989
(805) 461-1338
Spanish

Alliance Against Family Violence
Bakersfield
(800) 433-7337
(805) 327-1091
(805) 322-0931
Spanish, 3 Indian dialects

Interface Children, Family
Services
Camarillo
(800) 339-9597
(805) 485-6114
Spanish

Catalyst Women's Advocates
Chico
(800) 895-8476
(916) 895-8476
(916) 343-7711
Spanish, Hmog, Japanese

Center for the Pacific-Asian
Family, Inc.
Los Angeles
(800) 339-3940
(213) 653-4042
(213) 653-4045
*Asian-Indian, Thai, Chinese,
Japanese, Korean, Vietnamese*

Haven Women's Center of
Stanislaus
Modesto
(800) 834-1990
(209) 577-5980
(209) 576-0659
Spanish, Asian

Shelter from the Storm
Palm Desert
(800) 775-6055
(619) 328-SAFE
(619) 341-9785
Spanish

Alternatives to Domestic
Violence
Riverside
(800) 339-SAFE
(909) 683-0829
(909) 352-9262
Spanish

Shelter Plus
Salinas
(800) 339-8228
(408) 422-2201
(408) 442-3024
Spanish

Asian Women's Shelter
San Francisco
(415) 751-0880
(415) 751-7110
Mandarin, Korean, Cantonese,
Toisanese, Japanese, Tagalog,
Laotian, Mein, Vi

COLORADO

Family Crisis Services, Inc.
Canon City
(303) 275-2429
Spanish, German, ASL

Alternatives to Family Violence
Commerce City
(303) 289-4441
(303) 289-4473
Spanish, ASL, other interpreters

Denver Victims Service Center
(Not a shelter)
Denver
(303) 894-8000
(303) 860-0660
(303) 860-9555 TDD
Spanish

CONNECTICUT

The Umbrella Program
Arsonia
(203) 736-9944
(203) 736-2601
Interpreters are available

Prudence Crandall Center for
Women
New Britain
(203) 225-6357
(203) 225-5187
Polish, Spanish

Domestic Violence Services of
Greater New Haven
New Haven
(203) 789-8104
(203) 865-1957
Spanish

Domestic Violence Services, Inc.
Stamford
(203) 357-8162
Spanish, French, German,
Russian, Hebrew, Italian,
Ukrainian

DELAWARE

Families in Transition Center
People's Place II, Inc.
Milford
(302) 422-8058
(302) 422-8033
Spanish, Creole, interpreters
available

Battered Women's Hotline
Wilmington
(302) 762-6110
(302) 762-6111
Spanish

DISTRICT OF COLUMBIA

House of Imagene
(202) 797-7460

House of Ruth—"Herspace"
(202) 347-2777
(202) 347-0737
Spanish

My Sister's Place
(202) 529-5991
(202) 986-1476
Spanish

FLORIDA

Another Way, Inc.
Archer
(800) 369-6700
(904) 493-2522
Spanish

Shelter House, Inc.
Fort Walton Beach
(800) 44-ABUSE
(904) 863-4777
(904) 833-3772

Shelter for Abused Women
of C.C.
Naples
(800) 780-HELP
(813) 775-1101
(813) 775-3862
Spanish, Creole

Rape Crisis/Spouse Abuse
Center
Ocala
(800) 736-4461
(904) 622-8495
Spanish, Polish

Quigley House, Inc.
Orange Park
(800) 339-5017
(904) 284-0061
(904) 284-0340
Spanish

GEORGIA

Northwest Georgia Family Crisis
Center, Inc.
Dalton
(706) 278-6595
Spanish

Women's Resource Center of
DeKalb County
Decatur
(404) 688-9436
Spanish

S.H.A.R.E. House, Inc.
Douglasville
(800) 643-1212
(404) 489-7513

The Salvation Army Safe House
Warner Robins
(912) 923-6294
(912) 923-2348
Spanish, French, Latin

HAWAII

The Family Crisis Shelter, Inc.
Hilo
(808) 959-9955
Japanese, Singapore

Child and Family Service Shelter
for Abused Spouses
Honolulu
(808) 841-0822
(808) 847-4602
Filipino

Kauai YWCA Family Violence
Shelter
Lihue
(808) 245-6362
(808) 245-8404
Spanish, Filipino, Japanese

IDAHO

YWCA Women's and Children's
Crisis Center
Boise
(208) 343-7025
(208) 343-3688

Lewiston/Clarkston YWCA
Crisis Services
Lewiston
(800) 669-3176
(208) 746-9655
Spanish, Japanese

Upper Valley Help for Family
Violence
Rexburg
(800) 962-5601
(208) 624-3068
(208) 356-0065
Spanish interpreter

ILLINOIS

Mutual Ground, Inc.
Aurora
(708) 897-0080
(708) 897-8989
Spanish interpreter

Women's Crisis Center of
Metro East
Belleville
(800) 924-0096
(618) 235-0892
(618) 236-2531
Japanese

Rainbow House/Arco Iris
Chicago
(312) 762-6611
(312) 521-5501
TDD number (312) 762-7038

YWCA Women's Shelter
Danville
(217) 443-5566
(217) 446-1217
Translator for German, Spanish

Anna Bixby Women's Center
Harrisburg
(800) 421-8456
(618) 252-8389
(618) 252-8380
Spanish

Freedom House Domestic
Violence Shelter
Princeton
(800) 474-6031
(815) 875-8233
(815) 872-0087
Polish, German

INDIANA

YWCA Shelter for Women
Victims of Violence
Fort Wayne
(800) 441-4073
(219) 447-7233
Spanish

YWCA Family Intervention
Center
Kokomo
(800) 241-3041
(317) 459-0314
(317) 457-3293
Spanish

North Central Indiana Rural
Crisis Center, Inc.
Rensselaer
(800) 933-0374
(219) 866-8281
German, Spanish

IOWA

Council Against Domestic
Abuse
Cherokee
(800) 225-5003
(800) 225-7233
(712) 225-5003
*Laos, Spanish, German, Korean
interpreters*

Family Violence Center
Des Moines
(800) 942-0333
(515) 243-6147
Hispanic, Lastion, ASL

Domestic Violence Intervention
Pro.
Iowa City
(800) 373-1043
(319) 354-7840

KANSAS

The Family Life Center
Safe House
El Dorado
(800) 870-6967
(316) 321-7104
Spanish, ASL

S.O.S., Inc.
Emporia
(800) 825-1295
(316) 342-1870
Spanish

Domestic Violence Association
of Central Kansas
Salina
(800) 874-1499
(913) 827-5862
Spanish, Vietnamese

KENTUCKY

Barren River Area Safe Space
Spouse Abuse Center, Inc.
Bowling Green
(800) 928-1184
(502) 843-1182
Interpreters available

Sanctuary Inc.
Hopkinsville
(800) 766-0000
(502) 886-8174
(502) 885-4572
Interpreters available

YWCA Spouse Abuse Center
Lexington
(800) 544-2022
(602) 233-9927

Domestic Violence Emergency
Service
Morehead
(800) 221-4361
(606) 784-7980
(606) 784-7980

Big Sandy Family Abuse Center
Prestonburg
(800) 649-6605
(606) 285-9079
(606) 886-6025

LOUISIANA

Family Counseling Agency
Alexandria
(800) 960-9436
(318) 445-2022
(318) 442-7196

June Jenkins Women's Shelter
DeRidder
(800) 54-ABUSE
(318) 462-6504
(318) 462-1452
German, Spanish

Women's Shelter
Lake Charles
(800) 223-8066
(318) 436-4552
German, Spanish, Thai, French

YWCA of Monroe
Monroe
(800) 716-7233
(318) 323-4112
(318) 323-1505

MAINE

Abused Women's Advocacy
Project
Auburn
(207) 795-4020
(207) 784-3995
(800) 559-2927
French, Chinese, Cambodian

WomanKind, Inc.
Machias
(207) 255-4785
(207) 255-3031
(800) 432-7303
Nepalese, Spanish, ASL

Battered Women's Project
Presque Isle
(207) 769-8251
(207) 764-2977
(800) 439-2323
French

MARYLAND

Mid-Shore Council on Family
Violence, Inc.
Denton
(410) 822-5276
(410) 479-1149
(800) 927-HOPE
Spanish, ASL

Citizen's Assisting & Sheltering
the Abused CASA
Hagerstown
(301) 739-8975
(301) 739-4990
Spanish

Abused Persons Program/Calvert
County Health Dept.
Prince Frederick
(410) 535-1121
(410) 535-5400
(301) 855-1075
Spanish, Russian

MASSACHUSETTS

Casa Myrna Vazquez, Inc.
Boston
(617) 521-0100
(800) 992-2600
Spanish, French, Lakota

Women's Resource Center, Inc.
Lawrence
(508) 685-2480
(800) 400-4700
Spanish, Portuguese

The Support Committee for
Battered Women
Waltham
(800) 899-4000
(617) 891-0724
(800) 899-4000
Spanish, French, Portuguese

YWCA New Beginnings
Westfield
(413) 562-1920
(413) 562-5739
(800) 479-6245

MICHIGAN

Bay County Women's Center
Bay City
(517) 686-4551
(800) 834-2098
French, Spanish, Italian, ASL

Safe Shelter, Inc.
Benton Harbor
(616) 983-4275
(616) 925-2280
(800) 310-5454

Women's Information Service
Inc.
Big Rapids
(616) 796-6600
(616) 796-6692
(800) 374-WISE

Branch County Coalition
Against Domestic Violence
Coldwater
(517) 278-7432
Spanish

YWCA of Greater Flint
Domestic Violence/Sexual
Assault Services
Flint
(810) 236-7233
(810) 238-7621
ASL

YWCA Domestic Crisis Center
Grand Rapids
(616) 774-3535
(616) 459-4652

Women's Resource Center of
Northern Michigan, Inc.
Petoskey
(616) 347-0082
(616) 347-0067
(800) 275-1995
Have access to ASL, German,
Spanish, French, Italian

Eastern Upper Peninsula
Domestic Violence Program
Sault Ste. Marie
(906) 635-0566
(906) 635-0566
(800) 882-1515

St. Joseph County Domestic
Assault Shelter Coalition
Three Rivers
(616) 279-5122
(800) 828-2023

MINNESOTA

Houston County Women's
Resources
Caledonia
(507) 724-2676
(800) 362-8255
Spanish, German, ASL

Migrant Health Services Inc.
Crookston
(800) 342-7756
(218) 281-3552
(800) 660-6667
Spanish

Women's Crisis Center
Fergus Falls
(218) 739-3359
(218) 739-3486
(800) 974-3359
Spanish, ASL, Chinese

Family Violence Network
Lake Elmo
(612) 770-0777
(612) 770-8544
Interpreters available

Committee Against Domestic
Abuse
Mankato
(507) 625-SAFE
(507) 625-8688
(800) 477-0466
Spanish, Hmong, Laotian,
Russian, Vietnamese

Home Free Shelter
Plymouth
(612) 559-4945
(612) 559-9008

Women's Shelter Inc.
Rochester
(507) 285-1010
(507) 285-1938
(800) 438-6439
Chinese, Kerlan, Hmong,
Vietnamese, Laotian, Cambodian,
Spanish

Central MN Task Force on
Battered Women
St. Cloud
(612) 252-1603
(612) 253-6900
(800) 950-2203
Spanish, Swedish, German, Thai,
Hmong, Polish, Vietnamese,
Ukrainian, Laotian

Casa de Esperanza
St. Paul
(612) 772-1611
(612) 772-1723
Spanish, ASL

YWCA of St. Paul
St. Paul
(612) 222-3741
Spanish

Shelter House
Willmar
(800) 476-3234
(612) 231-9154
(800) 476-3234
Spanish, ASL

MISSISSIPPI

Gulf Coast Women's Center
Biloxi
(601) 435-1968
(601) 436-3809
(800) 800-1396
French, Arabic, Spanish, Sign Language, Vietnamese

Shelter for Battered Families
Catholic Charities
Jackson
(601) 366-0222
(601) 366-0750
(800) 273-9012

Catholic Charities Guardian
Shelter for Battered Families
Natchez
(601) 442-0142
(800) 273-6938

Domestic Violence Project, Inc.
Oxford
(601) 234-7521
(601) 234-5085
(800) 227-5764

Salvation Army Domestic
Violence Shelter
Pascagoula
(601) 762-8269
(601) 762-8267
(800) 382-7649

Haven House Family Shelter,
Inc.
Vicksburg
(601) 638-0555
(800) 898-0860

MISSOURI

Safe House for Women, Inc.
Cape Girardeau
(314) 651-1614
(314) 355-7745
ASL

Avenues
Hannibal
(314) 221-4280
(314) 221-2093
(800) 678-7713

Harbor Lights Shelter Program
from Domestic Violence
Kimberling City
(417) 739-2118
(800) 831-6863
Spanish, French

Council to Prevent Family
Violence of Laclede City
Lebanon
(417) 588-9773
(417) 532-2885
(800) 588-9773

Council on Families in Crisis
Nevada
(417) 667-3733
(417) 667-7171
(800) 398-4271
Interpreters available

Haven House, Inc.
Poplar Bluff
(314) 686-4873
(800) 491-1138

Family Violence Center, Inc.
Springfield
(417) 865-1728
(417) 865-0373
(800) 831-6863
*Spanish, French, German,
Vietnamese*

MONTANA

Bozeman Area Battered
Women's Network
Bozeman
(406) 586-4111
(406) 586-0263
(800) 834-8296
Crow, other interpreters available

Safe Space
Butte
(406) 782-8511
(406) 782-2111
(800) 479-8511

Violence Free Crisis Line
Kalispell
(406) 752-7273
(406) 752-4735
ASL

NEBRASKA

Center for Sexual Assault &
Domestic Violence Survivors
Columbus
(402) 564-2155
(800) 658-4482

Domestic Abuse/Sexual Assault
Crisis Center
Fremont
(402) 727-7777
(402) 721-4340
(800) 479-6221

Rape-Domestic Abuse Program
North Platte
(308) 534-3495
(308) 532-0624
Spanish

Haven House Family Services
Center
Wayne
(800) 440-4633
(402) 375-4633
(800) 440-4633

NEVADA

Advocates to End Domestic
Violence
Carson City
(702) 883-7654
(702) 883-7564
English, Spanish

Domestic Violence Intervention
Fallon
(702) 423-1313
(800) 500-1556
*Spanish, Filipino, interpreters
available*

Alternatives to Living in Violent
Environments
Yerington
(702) 463-4009
(702) 463-5843
(800) 465-4009
Spanish

NEW HAMPSHIRE

Response to Sexual & Domestic
Violence
Berlin
(800) 852-3388
(603) 752-2040
(800) 852-3388
French, Spanish, English

Rape & Domestic Violence
Crisis Center
Concord
(603) 225-7376
(800) 852-3388
Spanish, French, others available

A Safe Place
Portsmouth
(603) 436-7924
(800) 852-3388
*Spanish, German, French,
Laotian, ASL*

NEW JERSEY

Domestic Abuse & Rape Crisis
Belvidere
(908) 453-4181
(908) 453-4121
Translators available

Womanspace, Inc.
Lawrenceville
(609) 394-9000
(609) 394-0136
(800) 572-7233
Spanish

Women Aware, Inc.
New Brunswick
(908) 249-4504
(908) 249-4900
(800) 572-7233
*Spanish, German, Greek, Italian,
Russian, Indian, Polish, French*

Providence House—Ocean
County
Toms River
(908) 244-8259
(908) 244-6257
(800) 246-8910
Spanish

NEW MEXICO

Women's Community
Association
Albuquerque
(505) 247-4219
(800) 733-3645
Spanish

Carlsbad Battered Families
Shelter
Carlsbad
(505) 885-4615
(800) 439-7303
Spanish

Shelter for Victims of Domestic
Violence
Clovis
(505) 769-0305
(505) 762-0050
(800) 401-0305

La Casa, Inc.
Las Cruces
(505) 525-0371
(505) 526-2819
(800) 526-9513
Spanish

NEW YORK

Cayuga County Action Program
Auburn
(315) 253-3356
(315) 255-1703
(800) 942-6906
Spanish, French, Polish, ASL

The NET Domestic Violence
Program
Bath
(800) 286-3407
(607) 776-7664
(800) 346-2211
Interpreters available

Aegis Battered Women's
Program
Bronx
(212) 733-4440
Spanish

Transition Center
Far Rockaway
(718) 520-8045
(718) 327-7660
*Spanish, Hebrew, Russian,
Yiddish, Korean*

AMICAE, Inc.
Fredonia
(716) 672-8423
(800) 836-5940
*Spanish, French, Urdu, Bengali,
Hindi*

Neighborhood Justice Program
Hornell
(607) 962-6774
(607) 324-4433
(800) 346-2211

The Salvation Army Domestic
Violence Program
Jamestown
(716) 661-3897
(716) 483-0830
(800) 252-8748
Spanish

Family Domestic Violence
Services
Kingston
(914) 338-2370
(914) 331-7080

Community Action Agency of
Franklin County
Malone
(518) 483-1261
(800) 834-9474

STOP Domestic Violence
Plattsburgh
(518) 563-6904
(518) 563-8206
(800) 942-6906

The Salvation Army, Syracuse
Area Services
Syracuse
(315) 479-1332
(315) 475-1688
Spanish

My Sister's Place, Inc.
Tuckahoe
(914) 969-5800
(914) 779-3900
Spanish

NORTH CAROLINA

Roanoke-Chowan Services for
Abused Families
Ahoskie
(919) 332-1933
(919) 332-4047
(800) 669-1933

Davidson County Domestic
Violence Service, Inc.
Lexington
(704) 243-1628
(704) 243-1934
(800) 386-4124
Spanish, Thai, ASL, French

Helpmate of Madison, Inc.
Marshall
(704) 649-2446
(704) 649-2027
Interpreters available

Rainbow House
Rockingham
(910) 582-1935
Spanish

Hope Harbor Home
Supply
(919) 754-5856
(919) 754-5726
(800) SAY-HOPE

Crisis Council, Inc.
Troy
(910) 572-3747
(910) 572-3749
(800) 274-7471
Spanish

Domestic Violence Shelter &
Services
Wilmington
(910) 343-0703
(910) 343-9388
Spanish, French, Japanese

Family Services Shelter
Winston-Salem
(910) 723-8125
(910) 724-3979

NORTH DAKOTA

Abused Adult Resource Center
Bismarck
(800) 472-2911
(701) 222-8370
(800) 472-2911
German, Russian

Rape & Abuse Crisis Center of
Fargo/Moorhead
Fargo
(701) 293-7273
(800) 344-7273
Local translators

Adult Abuse Community
Service
Grand Forks
(701) 746-8900
(701) 746-0405
Spanish, Hebrew, Czech

Family Crisis Shelter
Williston
(701) 572-8412
(701) 572-0757

OHIO

House of Peace, Clermount
YWCA
Batavia
(513) 753-7281
(513) 753-7282
(800) 540-4764
Spanish, ASL

Haven of HOPE
Cambridge
(614) 432-3542
(614) 439-7233
(800) 304-HOPE
Spanish

First Step
Fostoria
(419) 435-7300
(800) 466-6228

Warren County Family Abuse
Shelter, Inc.
Lebanon
(513) 933-1107
(513) 933-2226
(800) 932-3366

The Domestic Violence Shelter
Inc.
Mansfield
(419) 374-5840
(800) 931-SAFE

Turning Point—Concerned
Citizens Against Violence
Against Women
Marion
(614) 382-8988
(614) 382-9192
(800) 232-6505
ASL, TDD number 614-383-1166

Women's Tri-County Help
Center
Saint Clairsville
(614) 695-1639
(614) 695-8774
(800) 695-1639
TDD, interpreters available

OKLAHOMA

ACMI House
Altus
(405) 482-3800
(405) 482-7449

Community Crisis Center
Miami
(918) 542-1001
(918) 540-2432
(800) 400-0883

Women's Resource Center
Norman
(405) 360-0590
(405) 364-9424
Spanish

KI BOIS Community Action
Foundation, Inc.
Stigler
(918) 967-3277
(918) 967-3325
(800) 299-4479

Help in Crisis, Inc.
Tahlequah
(918) 456-HELP
(918) 456-0673
(800) 300-5321
Cherokee, Spanish

OREGON

Central Oregon Battering &
Rape Alliance (COBRA)
Bend
(503) 389-8175
(503) 382-9227
(800) 356-2369
Spanish

Center Against Rape &
Domestic Violence
Corvallis
(503) 754-0110
(503) 758-0219
Spanish, Chinese, ASL

Lincoln Shelter & Services Inc.
Lincoln City
(503) 994-5959
(800) 841-8325

Dunn House
Medford
(503) 779-HELP
(503) 779-3960
(800) 5-HELP-01
Spanish

Coos County Women's Crisis
Services
North Bend
(503) 756-7000
(503) 756-7864
(800) 448-8125
Spanish, ASL

Domestic Violence Services
Pendleton
(503) 278-0241
(503) 276-3322
(800) 833-1161
Spanish

Battered Persons' Advocacy
Roseburg
(503) 440-4573
(503) 637-7867
(800) 464-6543
Spanish

PENNSYLVANIA

Turning Point of Lehigh Valley
Bethlehem
(610) 437-3369
(610) 867-6477
Spanish, Polish, German,
Chinese, Hungarian

Women's Center
Bloomsburg
(717) 784-6631
(717) 784-6632
(800) 544-8293
Interpreters available

Domestic Violence Services of
Cumberland County
Carlisle
(800) 852-2102
(717) 258-4806
(800) 852-2102
Spanish, ASL

YWCA of Greater Harrisburg
Harrisburg
(717) 238-7273
(800) 654-1211
Spanish

Alice Paul House
Indiana
(412) 349-4444
(800) 435-7249
ASL, French, Spanish, German

Women's Help Center, Inc.
Johnstown
(814) 536-5361
(800) 999-7406

Helping Abuse Victims in Need
Kittanning
(412) 548-8888
(412) 543-1180
(800) 841-8881
Interpreters available

Women in Crisis Carbon
County
Lehighton
(800) 424-5600
(610) 377-0760
(800) 424-5600
Czech, Italian, German, ASL,
Spanish, French

Schuylkill Women in Crisis
Pottsville
(717) 622-6220
(717) 622-3991
(800) 282-0634
Spanish, Chinese

Wise Options for Women
Williamsport
(717) 323-8167
(800) 326-8483
Polish, Russian

Access-York, Inc.
York
(717) 846-5400
(717) 845-8226
(800) 262-8444
Spanish

RHODE ISLAND

Sojourner House, Inc.
Providence
(401) 765-3232
(401) 861-6191
(401) 658-4334
Spanish

Women's Center of Rhode
Island
Providence
(401) 861-2760
Spanish, French, Portuguese,
Cambodian

Elizabeth Buffum Chase House
Warwick
(401) 738-1700
Spanish, Portuguese

SOUTH CAROLINA

Citizens Opposed to Domestic
Abuse
Beaufort
(803) 525-1009
(803) 525-9165
(800) 868-2332

Sistercare, Inc.
Columbia
(803) 765-9428
(803) 799-5477
(800) 637-7606
Persian

Pee Dee Coalition Against
Domestic & Sexual Assault
Florence
(803) 669-4694
(800) 273-1820
Spanish, hearing-impaired

My Sister's House Inc.
North Charleston
(803) 744-3242
(803) 747-4069
(800) 273-HOPE

Tri County CASA/Family
Systems
Orangeburg
(803) 531-6211
(803) 534-2272
Interpreters available

Sister Help
Rock Hill
(803) 329-2800
(803) 324-5141

Spartanburg County SAFE
Homes Network
Spartanburg
(803) 583-9803
(800) 273-5066

SOUTH DAKOTA

Sacred Heart Women's Shelter
Eagle Butte
(605) 964-7233
(605) 964-6062
Lakota

Fall River Crisis Intervention
Team, Inc.
Hot Springs
(605) 745-6070
(605) 745-5859
(800) 745-6070

Missouri Shores Domestic
Violence Center
Pierre
(605) 224-7187
(605) 224-0256
(800) 696-7187

Victims of Violence Intervention
Program
Spearfish
(605) 642-7825
(605) 642-9841
(800) 999-2348

Crisis Intervention Shelter
Service
Sturgis
(605) 347-0050
(800) 755-8432
Spanish, Lakota, German

TENNESSEE

HOPE—The Health,
Opportunity, Protection,
Encouragement Center
Athens
(615) 745-5289
*Spanish, French, Japanese,
hearing-impaired*

Battered Women, Inc.
Crossville
(615) 484-4642
(615) 456-0747
(800) 641-3434
Interpreters available

Women's Resource & Rape
Assistance Program (WRAP)
Jackson
(901) 664-9727
(800) 273-8712
Italian, Russian, Spanish, French

Families in Crisis Inc.
McMinnville
(615) 473-6221
(615) 473-6543
(800) 675-0766

CEASE (Community Effort
Against Spouse Abuse)
Morristown
(615) 581-2220
(615) 581-7029
(800) 303-2220
German, Spanish, Japanese, ASL

Safe Space/CCADV
Newport
(615) 623-3125
(615) 623-7734
(800) 244-5968
Spanish, German, ASL

TEXAS

Noah Project, Inc.
Abilene
(915) 676-7107
(800) 444-3551
Spanish

Family Support Services Rape
Crisis
Domestic Violence
Amarillo
(806) 373-8022
(806) 372-3202
(800) 749-9026
Spanish

Women's Center of Brazoria
County
Angleton
(409) 849-9553
(800) 243-5788
Spanish

Matagaorda County Women's
Crisis Center
Bay City
(409) 245-9299
(409) 245-9109
(800) 451-9235
Spanish

Women & Children's Shelter of
Southeast Texas
Beaumont
(409) 832-7575
(800) 621-8882
Spanish, French

Noah Project—Central Texas
Brownwood
(915) 643-2699
(800) 444-3551
Spanish

Women's Shelter of the Corpus
Christi Area, Inc.
Corpus Christi
(512) 881-8888
(512) 881-9674
(800) 580-HURT
Spanish

Denton County Friends
of the Family
Denton
(817) 382-7273
(817) 387-5131
(800) 572-4031
Spanish

Safe Place, Inc.
Dumas
(806) 935-2828
(806) 935-7585
(800) 753-7553
Spanish, Vietnamese

El Paso Shelter on Family
Violence
El Paso
(915) 593-7300
(915) 593-1000
(800) 727-0511
Spanish

Women in Need
Greenville
(903) 454-HELP
(903) 455-4612
(800) 7-HELP ME
Spanish, French, German

Cherokee County Crisis
Center, Inc.
Jacksonville
(903) 586-9118
(800) 232-8519
Spanish

Kilgore Community Crisis
Center
Kilgore
(903) 984-2377
(903) 984-3019
(800) 333-9148
Spanish

Families in Crisis
Killeen
(817) 634-8309
(817) 634-1184
(800) 373-2774
Spanish, German

Women's Protective Services of
Lubbock, Inc.
Lubbock
(806) 792-7295
(800) 736-6491
Spanish

Permian Basin Center for
Battered Women
Midland
(915) 570-1465
(915) 683-1300
(800) 967-8928
Spanish

HOPE
Mineral Wells
(817) 325-1306
(817) 325-1307
(800) 585-1306
Spanish, ASL

Women's Shelter of East Texas
Inc.
Nacogdoches
(409) 569-8850
(409) 569-1018
(800) 828-7233
Spanish

Family Haven Crisis & Resource
Center
Paris
(903) 784-6842
(800) 44-HAVEN
Spanish

Panhandle Crisis Center
Perryton
(806) 435-5008
(800) 753-5308
Spanish

Williamson County Crisis
Center
Round Rock
(512) 255-1212
(800) 460-7233
Spanish

Family Shelter & Referral
Service
San Angelo
(915) 655-5774
(800) 749-8631
Spanish

Guadalupe County Women's
Shelter
Seguin
(210) 372-2780
(800) 834-2033
Spanish

Crisis Center
Sherman
(903) 893-5615
(903) 893-3909
(800) 259-3909
Spanish

East Texas Crisis Center
Tyler
(903) 595-5591
(903) 595-3199
(800) 333-0358
Interpreters available

Family Abuse Center
Waco
(817) 772-8999
(800) 283-8401
Spanish, English, German

First Step, Inc.
Wichita Falls
(817) 692-1993
(817) 692-4494
(800) 658-2683
Spanish, ASL

UTAH

Color County Cottage Women's
Crisis Center
Cedar City
(801) 586-3842
(801) 865-7443
(800) 953-3842

The Center for Women &
Children in Crisis
Provo
(801) 377-5500
(801) 374-9351
Interpreters available

Women in Jeopardy Program
YWCA
Salt Lake City
(801) 355-2804
Spanish, Russian, ASL

VERMONT

Women's Crisis Center
Brattleboro
(802) 254-6954
(802) 257-7364
(800) 773-0689
ASL

Addison County Women in
Crisis
Middlebury
(802) 388-4205
Spanish

Clarina Howard Nichols Center
Morrisville
(802) 888-5256
(800) 498-5256
French, Spanish, German,
Chinese, Mandarin

Domestic Violence & Sexual
Assault Prevention Program
St. Albans
(802) 524-6575
(802) 524-6574
(800) 527-7748
French

VIRGINIA

Alexandria Domestic Violence
Program
(703) 838-4911
(800) 838-VADV
Spanish, other interpreters

Bethany House of North
Virginia
Falls Church
(804) 256-3526
(804) 998-8811
Hearing-impaired

HOPE House
Norton
(703) 679-7240
(800) 572-2278

Women's Resource Center of
the New River Valley
Radford
(703) 639-1123
(703) 639-9592
(800) 788-1123
Hearing-impaired

Franklin County Family
Resource Center
Rocky Mount
(703) 483-1234
(703) 483-5088
(800) 838-8238

Alternatives for Abused Adults
Staunton
(703) 886-6800
(703) 886-4001
(800) 56-HAVEN
Spanish, ASL

Samaritan House
Virginia Beach
(804) 430-2120
(804) 430-2642
(800) 838-VADV

The Haven
Warsaw
(804) 333-5433
(804) 333-5370
(800) 22-HAVEN
Spanish

Family Resource Center, Inc.
Wytheville
(703) 228-7141
(703) 228-8431
(800) 838-VADV
Vietnamese, Spanish

WASHINGTON

YWCA Alive Program
Bremerton
(206) 479-1980
(206) 876-1608
(800) 562-6025
Interpreters available

Human Response Network
Chehalis
(206) 748-6601
(800) 244-7414
Spanish, other interpreters

Snohamish County Center for
Battered Women
Everett
(206) 252-2873
(206) 259-2827
(800) 562-6025
*Spanish, Cambodian,
Vietnamese, ASL, Filipino*

Domestic Abuse Women's
Network (DAWN)
Kent
(206) 656-7867
(206) 656-4305
(800) 562-6025
Spanish, Mandarin, Chinese

Pacific County Crisis Support
Network
Naselle
(800) 435-7276
(206) 484-7191
(800) 562-6026

Safeplace: Rape Relief &
Women's Shelter Services
Olympia
(206) 754-6300
(206) 786-8754

Connections
Republic
(509) 775-3132
(509) 775-3307
Spanish, hearing-impaired

The Salvation Army/Hickman
House
Seattle
(206) 932-5341

Skamania County Council on
Domestic Violence
Stevenson
(509) 427-4210
(800) 562-6025
Spanish

YWCA Women's Support
Shelter
Tacoma
(206) 383-2593
(206) 272-4181
(800) 562-6025
Spanish, other interpreters

YWCA of Walla Walla
Walla Walla
(509) 529-9922
Spanish

WEST VIRGINIA

YWCA Resolve Family Abuse
Program
Charleston
(304) 340-3550
(800) 352-6513

Women's Aid in Crisis
Elkins
(304) 636-8433
(800) 339-1185

Branches Domestic Violence
Shelter
Huntington
(304) 529-2382
(800) 352-6513

Family Crisis Center
Keyser
(304) 788-6061
(800) 352-6513

Family Crisis Intervention
Center of Regim V, Inc.
Parkersburg
(304) 428-2333
(304) 428-3707
(800) 794-2335

YWCA Family Violence
Prevention Program
Wheeling
(304) 232-2748
(304) 232-0512
(800) 698-1247

WISCONSIN

Hope House
Baraboo
(608) 356-7500
(608) 356-9123
(800) 584-6790
TDD, Spanish

People Against a Violent
Environment
Beaver Dam
(414) 887-3785
(414) 887-3810
(800) 775-3785
Interpreters available

YWCA Family Shelter
Beloit
(608) 346-6391

YWCA Alternatives to Domestic
Violence
Janesville
(608) 752-2583
(608) 725-5445

Lac du Flambeau Domestic
Abuse Program
Lac du Flambeau
(715) 588-7660
(800) 236-7660

Time-Out Family Abuse Shelter
Ladysmith
(715) 532-7089
(715) 532-6976
(800) 924-0556

Rainbow House Domestic Abuse
Services, Inc.
Marinette
(715) 735-6656
(800) 956-6656
Spanish, others obtainable

Community Referral Agency
Inc.
Milltown
(715) 825-4404
(715) 825-4414
(800) 261-SAFE

Green Haven Family Advocates
Monroe
(608) 325-7711
(608) 325-6489
(800) 836-9788
*German, French, hearing-
impaired*

Family Advocates, Inc.
Platteville
(608) 348-3838
(608) 348-5995
(800) 924-2624

Passages, a Pro. for Survivors of
DV & SA, Inc.
Richland Center
(608) 647-3616
(608) 647-8775
(800) 236-4325
Hearing-impaired, Spanish

Turning Point for Victims of
Domestic Abuse, Inc.
River Falls
(715) 425-6751
(800) 338-2882
Spanish, ASL, others available

Advocates, Inc.
Saukville
(414) 284-6902
(414) 284-3577
(414) 375-4034
Hearing-impaired

Safe Harbor Domestic Abuse
Program
Sheboygan
(414) 452-7640
(414) 452-8611
(800) 499-7640
*Spanish, Hmong, hearing-
impaired*

Center Against Sexual and
Domestic Abuse, Inc.
Superior
(715) 392-3136
(800) 649-2921
*Hearing-impaired, others
available*

Family Center, Inc.
Wisconsin Rapids
(715) 421-1511
Hmong, ASL

WYOMING

Safe House/Sexual Assault
Services
Cheyenne
(307) 637-7233
(307) 634-8655
Spanish, German

Circle of Respect
Ethete
(307) 332-7046
(307) 332-3112

Sexual Assault & Family
Violence
Evanston
(307) 789-7315
(307) 789-3628
(800) 445-7233

The Turning Point, Lincoln
County Self-Help Center
Kemmerer
(307) 877-9209
(307) 877-6834

PUERTO RICO

Hogar Ruth
(809) 883-1884

San Vicente De Paul
San Juan
(809) 772-3744

U.S. VIRGIN ISLANDS

Women's Coalition of St. Croix
St. Croix
(809) 773-9272
Spanish, hearing-impaired

Women's Resource Center, Inc.
St. Thomas
(809) 776-7867
(809) 776-3966
Interpreters available

CANADA

National Association of Women
and the Law
(604) 1 Nicholas Street
Ottawa, Ontario, Canada KIN
787
(613) 241-7570
(613) 241-4657 (fax)

Lawyer Referral Service
(Canadian Bar Association)
#504 1148 Hornby Street
Vancouver, BC V6Z 2C3
(604) 687-3221
*Provides referral for legal
assistance*

Yukon Public Legal Education
Association
C/O Yukon College
Box 2799
Whitehorse, Yukon YIA 5K4
(403) 667-4305
(800) 668-5297 (information
line)
*Provides resources and
information to women*

Advocacy Access Project
#204 456 W. Broadway
Vancouver, BC V5Y 1R3
(604) 663-1278 (toll-free from
BC)
(604) 872-1278
*Provides comprehensive services
and resources for persons with
disabilities*

For information on:
—Wife Assault
—Family Problems? Where to
get help
—Income Assistance Appeals
—Welfare
—Living Common Law

*you can receive these publications
free of charge by writing to:*

Publications Clerk
Legal Services Society
Suite 300-1140 West Pender
Vancouver, B.C.
V6E 4G1

■

organizations

HELPING HANDS NATIONAL REFERRAL
TELEPHONE NUMBERS

ALCOHOLICS ANONYMOUS
*A network of mutual support groups for recovering alcoholics. See
your local telephone White Pages for local groups or call (212) 870-
3400*

AL-ANON FAMILY GROUP HEADQUARTERS
*Provides support for family and friends of alcoholics. Offers referrals and
a free information packet.*
(800) 356-9996

CENTERS FOR SUBSTANCE ABUSE TREATMENTS
*Provides information on drug abuse and on AIDS when related to drug
use. Offers referrals to drug and alcohol rehabilitation centers.*
(800) 662-4357
(880) 662-9832 (Spanish)

NATIONAL ASSOCIATION FOR PERINATAL ADDICTION RESEARCH AND EDUCATION
An organization focusing on addiction during pregnancy. Offers counseling and referrals.
(800) 638-2229

NATIONAL CLEARINGHOUSE FOR ALCOHOL AND DRUG INFORMATION
Provides referrals and resources, focuses on preventive and health-related information.
(800) 729-6686

NATIONAL BLACK WOMEN'S HEALTH NETWORK
An organization committed to defining, promoting, and maintaining the physical, mental, and emotional well-being of African American women. Provides information and referrals.
(800) 275-2947

NATIONAL CANCER INSTITUTE
Publishes information on a variety of topics related to breast cancer direction and treatment.
(800) 422-6237

Y-ME
A breast cancer support organization providing information hotline counseling, referrals, and brochures through a network of local chapters.
(800) 221-2141

CHILD ABUSE AND NEGLECT

CLEARINGHOUSE OF CHILD ABUSE AND NEGLECT INFORMATION
Provides information and publishes materials.
(800) 394-3366

NATIONAL COUNCIL ON CHILD ABUSE AND FAMILY VIOLENCE
Provides referrals to related agencies and shelters, as well as pamphlets on the various aspects of child abuse and family violence.
(800) 222-2000

NATIONAL RESOURCE CENTER ON CHILD ABUSE AND NEGLECT
Provides information and referrals to local services.
(800) 227-5242

PROGRAMS FOR ABUSIVE PARENTS

CHILD HELP USA
A crisis hotline providing information and referral to local resources available for both children and adults.
(800) 422-4453
(800) 422-4453 (hearing-impaired)

CUSTODY

COMMITTEE FOR MOTHER AND CHILD RIGHTS, INC.
An organization offering guidance and emotional support for mothers facing custody problems.
(703) 722-3652
Or write:
210 Old Orchard Drive
Clearbrook, VA 22624

PARENTS WITHOUT PARTNERS
(800) 637-7974

PARENTAL KIDNAPPING

CHILDFIND OF AMERICA
A network of individuals and groups serving as a contact point for separated children and parents; also publishes a newsletter.
(800) 426-5678

MISSING CHILDREN'S HELP CENTER
Shows photos nationwide for children missing, either because of parental or stranger abduction, or because they are runaways.
(800) 872-5437

NATIONAL CENTER FOR MISSING AND EXPLOITED CHILDREN
A clearinghouse for parents searching for missing children.
(800) 843-5678

PENSION RIGHTS CENTER
Publishes your pension rights at divorce: What women need to know.
(202) 296-3776

ASSOCIATION FOR CHILDREN FOR ENFORCEMENT OF SUPPORT
An organization to aid single parent families seeking lawful child support through information and advocacy change.
(800) 537-7072

HEALTH

NATIONAL WOMEN'S HEALTH NETWORK
Provides an information packet on lesbian health issues.
(202) 347-1140

NATIONAL HEADACHE FOUNDATION
Offers written information about the causes and treatment of headaches and can also provide a list of member physicians.
(800) 843-2256

NATIONAL INSTITUTE ON DEAFNESS AND OTHER COMMUNICATION DISORDERS
An institute of the National Institutes of Health which conducts and supports research in the areas of human communication. Established a national clearinghouse of information resources on the normal and disordered mechanisms of hearing, balance, taste, smell, voice, speech, and language. To receive information:
(800) 241-1044
(800) 241-1055 (hearing-impaired)

CDC NATIONAL AIDS HOTLINE
Provides information on HIV/AIDS, 24 hours a day.
(800) 342-2437
for additional information you can write:
CDC National AIDS Clearinghouse
Post Office Box 6003
Rockville, MD 20849-6003

OUT/REACH, INC.
HIV/AIDS support groups, education, prevention, testing, counseling.
(800) 441-2437

LUPUS FOUNDATION OF AMERICA
Provides a free information packet and support for people with lupus.
(800) 558-0121

EQUAL EMPLOYMENT OPPORTUNITY COMMISSION
Provides referrals to offices in other states.
(202) 275-7377

NATIONAL RESOURCES

NATIONAL COALITION AGAINST DOMESTIC VIOLENCE
National Hotline number (800) 799-7233 (24 hrs.)
(800) 787-3224 (TDD)

EQUIPMENT FOR EQUALITY
They provide legal and advocacy services to people with disabilities. They are located in every state in the U.S. To find the office in your state call:
(312) 341-0022
or you can write:
11 E. Adams, Suite 1200
Chicago, IL 60603

NATIONAL CLEARINGHOUSE ON MARITAL AND DATE RAPE
An organization active in research and public speaking that specializes in the issues of marital and date rape.
(510) 524-1582

NATIONAL ORGANIZATION FOR VICTIM ASSISTANCE
Publishes a newsletter, NOVA, and maintains a national directory of services for victims of all types.
(800) 879-6682

RESOURCE CENTER ON CHILD CUSTODY AND CHILD PROTECTION
Provides information, materials, consultation, technical assistance, and legal research related to child protection and custody within the context of domestic violence.
(800) 527-3223 (this is not a crisis service)

SALVATION ARMY
They provide emergency lodging, food, and shelter across America. See your Yellow Pages for the nearest location.

Or you can write:
Post Office Box 269
Alexandria, VA 22313

FEDERAL INFORMATION CENTER

(800) 366-2998
(800) 326-2996 (hearing-impaired)

SOCIAL SECURITY INFORMATION

(800) 772-1213
(800) 325-0778 (hearing-impaired)

NATIONAL RUNAWAY SWITCHBOARD

(800) 621-4000
(800) 621-0394 (hearing-impaired)

missing children state clearinghouse and parent locator numbers

STATE	STATE CLEARINGHOUSE	PARENT LOCATOR
Alabama	(205) 260-1100 (800) 228-7688	(202) 242-9300
Alaska	(907) 269-5497 (800) 478-9333	(907) 263-6280
Arizona	(602) 223-2158	(602) 252-4045 x351
Arkansas	(501) 682-1323	(501) 252-8178
California	(916) 227-3290 (800) 222-3463	(916) 227-3600
Colorado	(303) 239-4251 (303) 239-4222	(303) 866-5987 (303) 866-3353

Connecticut	(203) 238-6575	(203) 566-5438
Delaware	(302) 739-5883	(302) 577-4832
District of Columbia	(202) 576-6771	(202) 727-5046
		(202) 727-0376
Florida	(904) 488-5224	(904) 488-9907
	(800) 342-0821	
Georgia	(404) 244-2554	(404) 894-5933
	(800) 282-6564	
Illinois	(217) 782-6053	(217) 524-4568
	(800) 8843-5763	
Indiana	(317) 232-8310	(317) 232-4936
	(800) 831-8953	
Iowa	(515) 281-5138	(515) 281-8970
	(800) 346-5507	
Kansas	(913) 296-8200	(913) 296-1450
	(800) 572-7463	
Kentucky	(502) 227-8799	(502) 564-2244
	(800) 222-5555	x271
Louisiana	(504) 342-4011	(504) 342-5131
Maine	(207) 624-7097	(207) 289-2886
	(800) 452-4664	

Maryland	(410) 290-0780	(301) 333-0635
	(800) 637-5437	
Massachusetts	(617) 727-8972	(617) 727-4200
	(800) 622-5999	x363
Michigan	(517) 336-6603	(517) 373-8640

(This office is not a clearinghouse,
but an unofficial contact for
police assistance or leads.)

Minnesota	(612) 642-0610	(612) 297-1113
Mississippi	(601) 987-1592	(601) 354-6845
Missouri	(314) 751-3313	(314) 751-2464
	(800) 877-3452	
Montana	(406) 444-3625	(406) 657-6101
Nebraska	(402) 479-4019	(402) 471-9349
	(402) 479-4938	
Nevada	(702) 486-3420	(702) 687-4960
	(702) 486-3539	
New Hampshire	(603) 271-2663	(603) 271-4422
	(800) 852-3411	
New Jersey	(609) 882-2000	(609) 588-2355
	(800) 743-5377	

New Mexico	(505) 827-9187	(505) 827-7221

(This office is not a clearinghouse,
but an unofficial contact for
police assistance or leads.)

New York	(518) 457-6326	(518) 474-9092
	(800) 346-3543	
North Carolina	(919) 733-3914	(919) 571-4120
	(800) 522-5437	x226
North Dakota	(701) 224-2121	(701) 224-5486
	(800) 472-2121	
Ohio	(614) 644-0122	(614) 752-6567
	(800) 325-5604	
Oklahoma	(405) 848-6724	(405) 424-5871
		x2615
Oregon	(503) 378-3720	
	x4412	
	(503) 373-7300	
	(800) 282-7155	
Pennsylvania	(717) 783-5524	(717) 783-3032
Rhode Island	(401) 444-1125	(401) 464-3014
	(800) 286-8626	

South Carolina	(803) 737-9000 (800) 322-4453 (SC only)	(803) 737-5820
Tennessee	(615) 741-0430	(615) 741-7923
Texas	(512) 465-2814 (800) 346-3243	(512) 463-2181 x3334
Vermont	(802) 773-9101	(802) 241-2891
Virginia	(804) 674-2026 (800) 822-4453	(804) 662-9627
Washington	(206) 753-3960 (800) 543-5678	(206) 586-2679
Wyoming	(307) 777-7537	(307) 777-6067

NATIONAL CLEARINGHOUSES

Canada	(613) 993-1525
United States	(703) 235-3900 (800) 843-5678

OUTSIDE THE UNITED STATES

CHILD FIND CANADA
710 Dorval Drive
Suite 210
Oakville, Ontario, Canada L6K 3V7
(905) 845-9621
This agency has offices throughout Canada.

EUROPE
Missing Children International Network
Rue Defacqz 1
Box 23
1050 Brussels, Belgium
Phone: 02-534-6531
Fax: 32-2-7624195

about the author

SUSAN MURPHY-MILANO is the founder of Project:Protect, a nonprofit agency dedicated to helping victims of stalking and domestic violence. In 1993 she was instrumental in the passage of the Illinois stalking law and has consistently argued for the rights of battered women and children through legislation and through national television appearances and the print media.